This is quite the best of all the Lent books I've ever read. I just loved the way Amy takes us through the Bible, revealing God's forgiving heart and his burning desire that we should forgive one another.

Jennifer Rees Larcombe, *Journey into God's Heart*

Few topics are more central to the Christian life—and life in general—than forgiveness. In this Lenten guide, Amy Boucher Pye traces the forgiveness theme through the length and breadth of scripture, finding it in both expected and surprising places. Combining deep insight and practical exercises, *The Living Cross* will help you live free from offences both committed and suffered.

Sheridan Voysey, *Resurrection Year*

A fresh approach to the timeless necessity to remain healthy as a child of God. A book that helps you to bring forgiveness home to your heart and life.

Russ Parker, *Forgiveness Is Healing*

Reading this book was, for me, as if Amy had taken a highlighter pen to the Bible and skilfully brought colour and clarification to so many passages where forgiveness and hope are found. Every page is like another journey into the grace of God. Also, the prayers and creative responses are so helpful for both individuals and small groups. This really is a wonderful resource for the Lent season and beyond.

Cathy Madavan, *Digging for Diamonds*

Amy has a distinct knack of distilling great thought and insight into just a few words. Her study of the excerpts of both the Old and New Testaments will help any reader reflect on the concept of forgiveness in an age when this can be a struggle. Amy will lead you on a journey of discovery, where you will be led to the cross of Jesus Christ. You will be confronted by God's great generosity,

Rt Revd Rob Wickham, Bishop of Edmonton

A Lenten journey you won't want to miss. From the fall to the cross and beyond, Amy Boucher Pye walks us down the centuries to meet the one she calls the 'Father of outstretched arms'. With captivating writing and inspiring biblical insight, we are reassured from the stories of fallen heroes, fallible leaders and plain ordinary sinners that God's lavish forgiveness is available to each one of us. The more I read, the more excited I became, and the more thankful I am for God's 'scandalous grace and love poured out'. Simply superb. I can't wait to read it again!

Catherine Campbell, *Chasing the Dawn*

This book pleasantly surprised me. While it is essentially a book of daily reflections for Lent, it is also a sensitive probing of the painful experiences people face and how the love of God through Christ can transform situations. The writer explores the depth and breadth of pain and hurt in life for many, if not all. She crafts ancient biblical stories with contemporary experience and draws insightful spiritual lessons and principles. While each day's reflection is brief, there is depth in her understanding. The activities and questions mean this is a helpful resource for groups and individuals as well as hard-pressed clergy or worship leaders looking for new ways to walk familiar paths. This could be a good resource for a discipleship course—Lent or not. It carefully exposes the human condition of brokenness before God and also presents the way forward in Christ by the Spirit.

Dianne Tidball, *The Message of Women*

# The Living Cross

*Exploring God's gift of forgiveness and new life*

Amy Boucher Pye

BRF

**The Bible Reading Fellowship**
15 The Chambers, Vineyard
Abingdon OX14 3FE
**brf.org.uk**

The Bible Reading Fellowship (BRF) is a Registered Charity (233280)

ISBN 978 0 85746 512 2
First published 2016
10 9 8 7 6 5 4 3 2 1 0
All rights reserved

**Acknowledgements**
Unless otherwise stated, scripture quotations are taken from The Holy Bible, New International Version (Anglicised edition) copyright © 1979, 1984, 2011 by Biblica. Used by permission of Hodder & Stoughton Publishers, an Hachette UK company. All rights reserved. 'NIV' is a registered trademark of Biblica. UK trademark number 1448790.

Extracts from the Authorised Version of the Bible (The King James Bible), the rights in which are vested in the Crown, are reproduced by permission of the Crown's Patentee, Cambridge University Press.

Every effort has been made to trace and contact copyright owners for material used in this resource. We apologise for any inadvertent omissions or errors, and would ask those concerned to contact us so that full acknowledgement can be made in the future.

A catalogue record for this book is available from the British Library

Printed by Lightning Source

To my family—
forgiving and forgiven.

And to my friends
who for decades have
known, loved, and forgiven me.

Your love is
more precious than gold;
sweeter than honey.

# Contents

# Foreword

How many times have we said those familiar words as our Lord has commanded and taught us: 'Forgive us our trespasses as we forgive those who trespass against us'? Christ's message of forgiveness and reconciliation is at the heart of the gospel. His finished work upon the cross signals a new relationship with God and with one another, and new life in the Holy Spirit.

These 47 reflections carry us from Ash Wednesday and the fall in the garden of Eden, to Easter Day and the commissioning of a forgiven Peter. The stories and illustrations bring home the message of hope and of a forgiving God who so loved the world that he was generous and gave himself to us in the person of Jesus Christ.

Again and again, as Amy Boucher Pye takes us through scripture and the experiences of the saints of God, she reminds us that Jesus comes to us just as we are. The Spirit of God searches us and knows us better than we know ourselves, and accepts us, as we are, behind the various disguises that we wear. The apostle Paul rejoices that by the grace of God we are 'accepted in the Beloved'. That is why, at confirmation, we are anointed, as ancient kings and priests were anointed, with the oil of gladness and the words, 'Shine in the world as one of God's chosen ones, beloved and accepted in Jesus Christ our Lord.'

I trust and pray that you will have a blessed and holy Lent and that as you follow our Lord through the steps of his passion, you may come to rejoice with all the saints who find the living cross none other than the gate of heaven.

Remember us, O God, and shape our history,
form our inward eyes
to see the shadow of the life-giving cross
in the turbulence of our time;
for his sake who died for all,
Christ our Lord.

Common Worship Psalm 136, prayer of response

The Rt Revd and Rt Hon Dr Richard Chartres, Bishop of London

# Introduction

# The gift of forgiveness

The extraordinary scene, recounted years later by a then Jewish prisoner in a Nazi concentration camp, captures our attention:

> 'I know,' muttered the sick man, 'that at this moment thousands of men are dying. Death is everywhere. It is neither infrequent nor extraordinary. I am resigned to dying soon, but before that I want to talk about an experience which is torturing me. Otherwise I cannot die in peace.'[1]

Speaking was an SS officer to the prisoner, who had been made to work near the hospital where the officer lay dying and had been summoned into the sickroom, not knowing why. The man with a bandaged head breathed with a rattle and said that he had to speak of something dreadful and inhuman. 'I must tell you of this horrible deed—tell you because... you are a Jew.'

The prisoner didn't know what to think, wondering if this was a trap or if the German soldiers for whom he was working would realise he had left his post and punish him accordingly. He longed to leave the room, sitting 'like a cat on hot bricks' as he tried to release his hand from the officer's. Several times he tried to leave, but the officer asked him to stay as he detailed how he had volunteered for the Hitler Youth and had become involved in the SS.

Then the dying man started to share about the deed weighing on his conscience. He and some other soldiers had been ordered to gather up some 200 Jewish people into a small house. Once they had herded them into this dwelling, the soldiers were ordered to throw grenades in through the open windows: 'We heard screams and saw the flames eat their way from floor to floor...'

The story was all too familiar to the prisoner, a man who had become immune to death as he witnessed it daily. Still, he felt horror at the officer's words and tried to leave, but again the officer begged him to stay, saying:

> I cannot die… without coming clean. This must be my confession… I know that what I have told you is terrible. In the long nights while I have been waiting for death, time and time again I have longed to talk about it to a Jew and beg forgiveness from him… I know that what I am asking is almost too much for you, but without your answer I cannot die in peace.

The prisoner writes:

> What a contrast between the glorious sunshine outside and the showdown of this bestial age here in the death chamber! Here lay a man in bed who wished to die in peace—but he could not, because the memory of his terrible crime gave him no rest. And by him sat a man also doomed to die—but who did not want to die because he yearned to see the end of all the horror that blighted the world.

> Two men who had never known each other had been brought together for a few hours by Fate. One asks the other for help. But the other was himself helpless and able to do nothing for him.

> I stood up and looked in his direction… At last I made up my mind and without a word I left the room.

The prisoner wasn't able or willing to forgive, but afterwards he couldn't stop wondering if he should have done. His friends in the camp had differing opinions, and he ends his book by asking the provocative question, 'What would you have done?'

We'll look at the answer to that question this Lent in varying forms as we explore the gift of forgiveness, and how at the cross of Christ we can find freedom and new life. As we ponder the question of whether or not we can forgive, we realise that forgiveness itself is radical: not everyone avails themselves of this gift. But through the sacrificial death of Jesus on the cross we can be free, for no longer does sin need to cloud our lives and twist our relationships.

Christians have been so schooled in the idea of forgiveness—it is, after all, a basic tenet of our faith—that we can become complacent. Through negligence or disuse we may avoid modelling forgiveness to our neighbour and become weighed down by the arguments, recriminations and hurts we inflict and receive. But God through his Son and Spirit wants to release us from an enslavement to sin, hurt and bitterness.

Lent is traditionally a time of self-examination and thus an opportune moment to delve into God's stories of forgiveness. As we move from Ash Wednesday to Easter Day we will engage with biblical characters from both the Old Testament and the New, as well as modern-day accounts of sin and forgiveness.[2] Through the reading, reflection, prayers and exercises, I hope we will come to understand not only in our heads but in our hearts the profound gift we have received by Jesus' death. We will come to see the living power of the cross, at which we exchange our hurtful thoughts and actions for God's love, grace and forgiveness.

Each day we engage with scripture before finishing with a prayer, and for each week I've included some questions for reflection and discussion and several practical spiritual exercises to help bring the scriptures alive. The exercises have been created with the individual in mind, but they can be adapted for use in small groups. Note that you may wish to skip ahead to the exercises during the week, and also note that the first exercise, where we come to the living cross for forgiveness and release, can be practised fruitfully throughout Lent.

The six weeks (plus the four days from Ash Wednesday to Saturday) have been equally divided between the Old and the New Testaments. We start, in our extended Week 1, with the founders of our faith—fallen heroes such as Adam and Eve, Abraham, Isaac, Jacob and Moses. We begin with God's creation and the quick fall of humanity into sin and death, after which the world is never the same. But the Lord loves his people and promises through the covenant that he will always be their God. The number of times they fail reveals their need for forgiveness.

In Week 2 we move to the kings, flawed but forgiven. The prophet Samuel anoints the first king, Saul, who turns out not to be the kind of king the Lord intends. Then of course comes David, someone the Lord calls a man after his own heart (1 Samuel 13:14), but a man who sins terribly. In Week 3 we look at the prophets, including Isaiah, Jeremiah, Daniel and Hosea. We see how they call God's people back to him through his message of judgement and mercy.

Halfway through Lent, in Week 4, we encounter Jesus, who preaches his radical message of forgiveness as he heals the sick and drives out demons. We see how his message divides the people and the religious leaders, but he is not deterred. We save the world-altering climax of Jesus' passion for Holy Week, so in Week 5 we jump ahead to the early church. We see a changed man in Peter, who at Pentecost preaches boldly to the thousands gathered, as well as Stephen, who later gives his eloquent testimony before being stoned to death. Saul's conversion is equally astonishing, as well as his teaching in his letters. He lives the rest of his days as an embodied example of one who is forgiven and free.

Then during Holy Week we return to Jesus and the momentous events from Palm Sunday through Maundy Thursday and Good Friday to Resurrection Sunday. That a man who was God would come to live as one of us and bear our sins to be the complete sacrifice boggles our minds and strikes love and gratitude into our hearts. On his cross he ushers in forgiveness and new life.

Before we delve into the readings, I leave you with a quotation that sums up our living cross. It's been attributed to St John Chrysostom, but was probably written by an unknown preacher in the fifth century:

This Tree is my eternal salvation. It is my nourishment and my banquet. Amidst its roots I cast my own roots deep: beneath its boughs I grow and expand, revelling in its sigh as in the wind itself. Flying from the burning heat, I have pitched my tent in its shadow, and have found a resting-place of dewy freshness. I flower with its flowers; its fruits bring perfect joy—fruits which have been preserved for me since time's beginning, and which now I freely eat. This Tree is a food, sweet food, for my hunger, and a fountain for my thirst; it is a clothing for my nakedness; its leaves are the breath of life. Away with the fig-tree, from this time on! If I fear God, this is my protection; if I stumble, this is my support; it is the prize for which I fight and the reward of my victory. This is my straitened path, my narrow way; this is the stairway of Jacob, where angels pass up and down, and where the Lord in very truth stands at the head.

This Tree, vast as heaven itself, rises from earth to the skies, a plant immortal, set firm in the midst of heaven and earth, base of all that is, foundation of the universe, support of this world of men, binding-force of all creation, holding within itself all the mysterious essence of man. Secured with the unseen clamps of the spirit, so that, adjusted to the Divine, it may never bend or warp, with foot resting firm on earth it towers to the topmost skies, and spans with its all-embracing arms the boundless gulf of space between.[3]

May we find forgiveness and new life at the foot of the living cross.

# Week 1

# Fallen Heroes:
# The Israelite Founders

In our journey of exploring the living cross as the source of forgiveness and new life, we start on Ash Wednesday at the very beginning, when it all goes wrong as Adam and Eve turn from God. From the start, we see our need for a Saviour, for Jesus to become the new Adam who leads us into life eternal.

We move next to sibling relationships and sibling rivalry, a tearing-apart between brothers that unfortunately continues through the generations, reflecting our need for Jesus' work on the cross. Then we come to our first fallen-but-redeemed founders of the faith, Abram and Sarai, who act on their fears through deception (Abram) and by turning to their own ways of making things happen (Sarai) instead of trusting God. Yet the Lord saves them and fulfils his promises, just as he made good on saving us from the curse of the law.

We encounter more sibling strife with Jacob and Esau, including parents who favour one child over the other and the destruction that follows. And yet God's redemptive work in Jacob brings harmony and reconciliation, hinting at the restored relationships we enjoy at the foot of the cross. Yet more unhappy families greet us in the stories of Joseph and his brothers, but we see also how God redeems the sin and deceit as Joseph saves his family and God's people from destruction through famine. So too does Jesus save us.

Our extended week ends with Moses, another great leader of God's people. He, a murderer, is still used by God as his instrument to lead his people to the promised land. We, like Moses, are made new at the living cross, where we can leave behind the old self as we put on the clothes of the new.

# Ash Wednesday

# First sins

Now the snake was more crafty than any of the wild animals the Lord God had made. He said to the woman, 'Did God really say, "You must not eat from any tree in the garden"?'

The woman said to the snake, 'We may eat fruit from the trees in the garden, but God did say, "You must not eat fruit from the tree that is in the middle of the garden, and you must not touch it, or you will die."'

'You will not certainly die,' the snake said to the woman. 'For God knows that when you eat from it your eyes will be opened, and you will be like God, knowing good and evil.'

When the woman saw that the fruit of the tree was good for food and pleasing to the eye, and also desirable for gaining wisdom, she took some and ate it. She also gave some to her husband, who was with her, and he ate it. Then the eyes of both of them were opened, and they realised that they were naked; so they sewed fig leaves together and made coverings for themselves.

GENESIS 3:1–7

They take and eat, and life will never be the same again.

Adam and Eve's eyes open after eating from the tree of the knowledge of good and evil, and they know more than God intends them—and us—to know. Though the fruit looks pleasing, consuming it results in the worst stomach ache ever. But they aren't left in the garden alone, helpless and hopeless, for the Lord God loves them and enacts a remedy—his grand rescue plan.

We start our Lenten journey of exploring the gift of forgiveness and new life with the fall of humanity, for when our first parents disobey God, the world changes for ever. This side of heaven, never again will we live in complete peace and harmony. Never again will we enjoy shame-free communion with our Maker or each other. Never again will we fully escape wrongful desire, severe labour or painful toil. We need the grace that God's forgiveness imparts.

Thus we need a Saviour, for Adam and Eve's turning from God ushers in repeat performances of disobedience down the ages, starting with their own duelling sons and continuing through the daughters and sons to follow: Abraham, Isaac, Jacob, Joseph, Moses and so on. They are heroes of our faith, but imperfect ones. For instance, in fear Abraham passes off his wife as his sister; Isaac favours one son over another; Jacob steals his brother's rightful blessing; Joseph lords his special position over his brothers; and Moses wrongfully kills an Egyptian. The list continues.

But God in his gracious mercy provides the solution to our dilemma when he sends his only Son to die in our place, redeeming us from the curse of the law (see Galatians 3:10–14). No longer do we need to be separated from God through our sins and wrongdoing, but we can be restored to a right relationship with him through Jesus' sacrifice. The cross is therefore a living place of exchange: the blood of Jesus removes the stain of our wrongdoing and imparts to us freedom and new life.

Although we are forgiven in the sense of being justified, we still need to forgive others and be forgiven by them and God. At the cross we can name our wrongful behaviour and impure thoughts and ask for God's forgiveness. As we confess our sins, one by one, God will forgive us and bring us freedom and release. And there we can take those wrongs committed against us, that they may no longer hold and shape us.

As we embark on exploring biblical stories of wrongs committed and forgiveness bestowed, may we grow in love for the triune God—Father, Son and Holy Spirit. May our journey to the cross and resurrection bestow on us an abiding sense of faith, hope and love. And may the spiritual disciplines we undertake during this journey bring about in us a renewed sense of wonder and gratitude for Jesus' great gift of death and new life: 'For as in Adam all die, so in Christ all will be made alive' (1 Corinthians 15:22).

## Prayer

*Loving Lord, the world is not as you created it. When Adam and Eve turned their faces from you in disobedience, sin and sickness entered in. But you sent your Son to die in my place, moving me from a place of death to new life. Please strengthen my understanding of and love for you during this grace-filled journey. In your time, reveal the areas where I need to relinquish control or confess my wrongdoing. I am humbled by your sacrifice, Lord Jesus. Thank you for making me clean.*

## Thursday

# Sibling rivalry

The Lord looked with favour on Abel and his offering, but on Cain and his offering he did not look with favour. So Cain was very angry, and his face was downcast.

Then the Lord said to Cain, 'Why are you angry? Why is your face downcast? If you do what is right, will you not be accepted? But if you do not do what is right, sin is crouching at your door; it desires to have you, but you must rule over it.'

Now Cain said to his brother Abel, 'Let's go out to the field.' While they were in the field, Cain attacked his brother Abel and killed him.

Then the Lord said to Cain, 'Where is your brother Abel?'

'I don't know,' he replied. 'Am I my brother's keeper?'

The Lord said, 'What have you done? Listen! Your brother's blood cries out to me from the ground. Now you are under a curse and driven from the ground, which opened its mouth to receive your brother's blood from your hand. When you work the ground, it will no longer yield its crops for you. You will be a restless wanderer on the earth.'

GENESIS 4:4B–12

'I love one son more than another,' said a mother in the weekend supplement of a national newspaper. The favourite son resembled her in disposition and physical features, so she could easily gauge what he was feeling in new or stressful situations. Because they were so similar, they clicked. As her other son closely resembled her ex-husband, she found his reactions and preferences foreign. Relating to him was more of a challenge.

Not surprisingly, the writer remained anonymous, for she felt ashamed to harbour favouritism between her sons. But she also couldn't see herself changing, and accepted the situation with fatalism, assuming that preferring a special child was a guilty secret widely shared. She justified her favouritism by saying that she came down harder on the favoured son, pushing him to succeed, while the lesser son got off more easily and enjoyed more freedom.

We don't know if Eve preferred Abel over Cain, and neither do we know why the Lord looked on Abel's sacrifice with favour but not Cain's, for the author of Genesis keeps a tight focus in his narrative. But Cain's response is clear when his steaming anger makes him want to kill his brother. He gives in to his rage, even though the Lord warns him to rule over the sin that's crouching outside his door. Having witnessed the crime, the Lord delivers the curse: Cain is banished from God's presence and will struggle to work the land. As we see in this story, Adam and Eve's sin ushered in yet more sin, and in just one generation it morphed into anger, jealousy, lying and premeditated murder. Welcome to life east of Eden.

Sibling rivalry goes deep, like an insidious weed that can choke off new sprigs of life. When children are young, it can grow with even the slightest permission, thus embedding itself in the roots of the plant. The circumstances that set it off could be innocent, such as having a sick child who needs continued medical attention and therefore takes more of the parent's time, or the preferences could be more deliberate, as in the case of the anonymous mother above. Unless we pull out the root of rivalry, however, the weed will suck nourishment out of its host. The key to removing the errant weeds is harder than it may sound: it's forgiveness.

Cain killed his opportunity to be forgiven by Abel, but God lessened Cain's punishment after he cried out for mercy. Although Cain deserved death, he lived, albeit with struggle and wandering. The Lord also gave Adam and Eve another son, Seth, to comfort them after Abel had died. The first family was broken, but God's mercy brings hope.

## Prayer

*Heavenly Father, how you must grieve at the broken relationships in families. You made us for each other, intending that any siblings or cousins would be a rich resource of love, care and shared history. For the strong family relationships that I enjoy or observe, I'm grateful. Please make these bonds stronger, that they would provide a haven of love and security. Where my family has been torn in two by jealousy, anger, curses or threats, please plant seeds of love and compassion, and in time bring your healing love and grace. Help me to remove any weeds of sin that choke out your nutrients, that your plants may grow into healthy trees which provide shade and fruit.*

# Friday

# The cost of deception

As [Abram] was about to enter Egypt, he said to his wife Sarai, 'I know what a beautiful woman you are. When the Egyptians see you, they will say, "This is his wife." Then they will kill me but will let you live. Say you are my sister, so that I will be treated well for your sake and my life will be spared because of you.'

When Abram came to Egypt, the Egyptians saw that Sarai was a very beautiful woman. And when Pharaoh's officials saw her, they praised her to Pharaoh, and she was taken into his palace. He treated Abram well for her sake, and Abram acquired sheep and cattle, male and female donkeys, male and female servants, and camels.

But the Lord inflicted serious diseases on Pharaoh and his household because of Abram's wife Sarai. So Pharaoh summoned Abram. 'What have you done to me?' he said. 'Why didn't you tell me she was your wife? Why did you say, "She is my sister," so that I took her to be my wife? Now then, here is your wife. Take her and go!' Then Pharaoh gave orders about Abram to his men, and they sent him on his way, with his wife and everything he had.

GENESIS 12:11–20

Hunger and fear can drive our lives in unwanted directions. Because of them, we may yearn for love, success, achievement, recognition, affirmation, security or acceptance. These emotions can push us to unhealthy relationships or to addictive behaviours that keep us from doing the right thing or from stepping out in faith. Fear might prevent us from acting on a divine nudge or from pursuing life-changing actions, such as breaking off an unsuitable relationship, searching for a new job or helping out with a church programme.

Abram isn't immune to these emotions. Following the Lord's commands, he moves to Canaan, the promised land, for the Lord has said that he will become a great nation and that everyone on earth will be blessed through him (Genesis 12:1–3). But when famine strikes, out of hunger Abram moves his family and his flocks to Egypt, where the regular flooding of the River Nile provides fertile land and more food. As far as we can tell, Abram doesn't consult the Lord before embarking on this journey.

When they reach Egypt, he acts out of self-interest and fear when he tells Sarai to pretend she's his sister so as to enter Pharaoh's good graces. He prostitutes his very own wife to gain favour with the foreign authorities. I wonder how the story would have ended if God hadn't intervened by sending disease to Pharaoh's household. But Abram repents; perhaps his conscience is pricked by Pharaoh's incredulous questioning about why he would pass off his wife as his sister. As it turns out, the foreign monarch has a higher moral code than Abram.

Abram leaves Egypt, going back to the place where he worshipped the Lord at Bethel, and again he calls on the name of the Lord (Genesis 13:3–4). I'm guessing he pours out his heart to God, confessing that he was wrong not to trust him and saying what a mess he's made, especially in his marriage. God restores him and Sarai, even allowing them to leave Egypt with all that Abram has acquired through the bride price extracted from Pharaoh (12:16).

We too might royally mess things up in our lives. We might let fear and hunger drive us to do the things we don't want to do. But the Lord promises to be with us moment by moment, helping us to face the fears and turn from them as we rest in his presence. He gives us the power to stand and resist, for we know he loves us unceasingly.

Although we still may reap the effects of our sin—whether through having to get out of debt or lose the excess weight or clean up our imaginations—God steps in and saves us from destruction. When we return to him, he brings healing and restoration and blessing, just as he did for Abram and his family.

## Prayer

*Heavenly Father, I'm humbled that you redeem fallen heroes, such as Abram. He became the father of many nations, but he deceived and lied, and didn't look to you. Release me from my fears, for I know that you are a loving, living Lord who will never leave me. And please keep me honest. Warn me through your Holy Spirit when I descend into wrongdoing, whether through self-deception, giving into impulses or fear-driven actions. Strengthen my resolve through your Holy Spirit and fill me with your indwelling presence, that I might collaborate with you, ushering in your kingdom.*

## Saturday

# From whence our help comes

Now Sarai, Abram's wife, had borne him no children. But she had an Egyptian slave named Hagar; so she said to Abram, 'The Lord has kept me from having children. Go, sleep with my slave; perhaps I can build a family through her.'

Abram agreed to what Sarai said. So after Abram had been living in Canaan ten years, Sarai his wife took her Egyptian slave Hagar and gave her to her husband to be his wife. He slept with Hagar, and she conceived.

When she knew she was pregnant, she began to despise her mistress. Then Sarai said to Abram, 'You are responsible for the wrong I am suffering. I put my slave in your arms, and now that she knows she is pregnant, she despises me. May the Lord judge between you and me.'

'Your slave is in your hands,' Abram said. 'Do with her whatever you think best.' Then Sarai ill-treated Hagar; so she fled from her.

The angel of the Lord found Hagar near a spring in the desert; it was the spring that is beside the road to Shur. And he said, 'Hagar, slave of Sarai, where have you come from, and where are you going?'

'I'm running away from my mistress Sarai,' she answered.

Then the angel of the Lord told her, 'Go back to your mistress and submit to her.' The angel added, 'I will increase your descendants so much that they will be too numerous to count.'
GENESIS 16:1–10

I announced to my boss and my colleagues that I was relocating halfway across the country—before I had a firm job offer or a place to live. When the plans fell through with an almighty thump, I had to ask humbly if I could stay on at my position. The leaders of the organisation welcomed me back warmly, but I'll never forget the sting of shame that I had given in so hugely to my 'leap before you look' tendencies. This experience and others have instilled in me the desire to learn from my reckless actions and to slow down and listen to the Lord.

Abram and Sarai are still waiting on God, and Sarai in particular wants to move along the process of producing an heir for Abram. Though we may find the notion of her suggesting that Abram produce a son through his slave-girl surprising or shocking, in the ancient Near East this practice was not only accepted but in places put into law.[4] As the process of conception wasn't yet understood, people then believed that the key ingredient in a child's birth was the man's sperm, with the woman merely providing a womb in which to foster the growth of the baby.[5] Thus whether Sarai or Hagar carried the child was less important than ensuring that an heir would be born, and as they had waited ten years already, Sarai yearned to see the promise realised.

But what happens next doesn't surprise us, for when Hagar conceives, the relationships change and jealousy and strife settle in. Hagar moves from being a servant to being the mother of the promised son (or so they think), and soon she despises Sarai, she of the barren womb. Sarai enlists Abram's help, but he escapes the conflict by saying that Sarai can settle matters herself. Her way of doing so sends Hagar fleeing to the desert, hardly a haven of safety. Taking matters into their own hands, Sarai and Abram put the well-being of the heir at risk.

The Lord sends a messenger to Hagar, telling her to return to Sarai and that she will be the mother of many. Then we see in the next chapter of Genesis God's gracious restatement of his covenant promise to Abram, that he will bear a son through his wife Sarai, and that his name will change from Abram, 'noble father', to Abraham, the 'father of many'. In addition, his wife's name will move from Sarai, 'princess', to Sarah, the 'mother of nations'.

What does this story have to do with forgiveness? After all, we don't see in the text how relationships are restored as the perpetrators repent of their sins and ask the victim to forgive them. But what many Christians miss—myself included, before I examined this issue in more depth—is that forgiveness in the Old Testament comes from the Lord, and that people aren't required to forgive one another.[6] The idea of a person forgiving another person becomes prominent only in the New Testament, with the sacrificial work of Jesus.

So as we see here, the Lord intervenes, bringing healing, restoration and forgiveness to this family. He is the one who reinstates Hagar and promises her an inheritance; he is the one who later renews his covenantal promises with Abram and Sarai—though they will need to wait more than another decade to see those promises come to fruition. From him flows new life and restored relationships.

Although through Jesus' death on the cross we can extend forgiveness to those who wrong us, we know that God is the source of all release from our sins. He is the one who makes forgiving possible, for he fills us with his grace and strengthens our will so that we can take the first step towards forgiving. As we ponder who we are in his universe, we can give thanks and rejoice in the way he orders our world.

## Prayer

*Father God, our Creator and Maker, I so regret it when I mess up my relationships. I get jealous and try to bend others to my will. I get frustrated and put up my hands while saying to another, 'You sort it out.' I get close to losing heart, running to the wilderness to hide, sometimes even feeling I want to die. But you love me and want the best for me. You want me to thrive, and sometimes that means waiting according to your timeline. Help me to wait; help me to love; help me to forgive. May your love oil the wheels of communication in my relationships, that the world may see your redeeming grace through me.*

# Sunday

# Unhappy families

After Isaac finished blessing him, and Jacob had scarcely left his father's presence, his brother Esau came in from hunting. He too prepared some tasty food and brought it to his father. Then he said to him, 'My father, please sit up and eat some of my game, so that you may give me your blessing.'

His father Isaac asked him, 'Who are you?'

'I am your son,' he answered, 'your firstborn, Esau.'

Isaac trembled violently and said, 'Who was it, then, that hunted game and brought it to me? I ate it just before you came and I blessed him—and indeed he will be blessed!'

When Esau heard his father's words, he burst out with a loud and bitter cry and said to his father, 'Bless me—me too, my father!'

But he said, 'Your brother came deceitfully and took your blessing.'

Esau said, 'Isn't he rightly named Jacob? This is the second time he has taken advantage of me: he took my birthright, and now he's taken my blessing!' Then he asked, 'Haven't you reserved any blessing for me?'…

Esau held a grudge against Jacob because of the blessing his father had given him. He said to himself, 'The days of mourning for my father are near; then I will kill my brother Jacob.'

GENESIS 27:30–36, 41

'All happy families are alike; each unhappy family is unhappy in its own way.' So begins Leo Tolstoy in his extended look at family life in *Anna Karenina*, revealing the reality of domestic bliss—with its imperfections—through the married couple Levin and Kitty rather than through the character bearing the novel's name. Tolstoy allows us to see not only the rewards of family life but also the heartbreak of a broken marriage.

Of course, Tolstoy's novel was preceded by stories of unhappy families going back to the first sons in the Bible, as we saw on Ash Wednesday. Today we read of another set of squabbling siblings, Jacob and Esau, whose conflict was intensified by their mother Rebekah.

The account in Genesis tells how as Isaac prepares to die, he asks his elder son, Esau, to make him his favourite meal so that he might bless him. When Rebekah overhears the plans, she schemes so that their younger son, Jacob, will receive the blessing. Why does she do such a thing? Perhaps she's motivated by the Lord's words when she was pregnant with the twins: 'The elder will serve the younger' (Genesis 25:23). She may believe that Isaac will prevent the Lord's will if he blesses the wrong son, so she sets her plan in motion.

Rebekah's arrangements result in Jacob deceiving his father and receiving his brother's blessing—the one Esau had relinquished earlier when he sold his birthright for a tasty bowl of stew (Genesis 25:29–34). But Rebekah hasn't reckoned on the unintended consequences of her deception, namely her sons being set against each other, with Esau planning his brother's death and Jacob having to flee to escape Esau's wrath. As she prepares to become a widow, she also loses daily contact with her favourite son.

It's uncomfortable to sit with the feelings that emerge when we think about lies, stealing and deviousness within family life. We see the ripple effect of the actions of previous generations spreading out to later generations, and we might feel helpless and hopeless. How, we wonder, can the Lord bring his mercy, grace and peace to dwell with us in these places of pain?

We have no easy answers, but we trust that the Lord can work his will in our lives, and that we can be free from the sins of the generations before us through the cross of Christ. Through his loving sacrifice and the power of the Holy Spirit, he can reverse the state of unhappy families.

## Prayer

*Father God, you are the Father of all. You have made me and formed me and in you I live and move and have my being. Lord, so often I rue the mess I've made of my family life—the sadness, the pain, the disappointment. Only you can bring healing and forgiveness. Only you can release me, through the power of the cross, from my sins and from those done against me. Please help me when I find myself in tough situations, about which you know fully. As you work your grace, may I look to you with praise and thanksgiving, knowing that you love me, and that you love it when your children love each other.*

## Monday

# Tearful reunion

Then Jacob prayed, 'O God of my father Abraham, God of my father Isaac, Lord, you who said to me, "Go back to your country and your relatives, and I will make you prosper," I am unworthy of all the kindness and faithfulness you have shown your servant. I had only my staff when I crossed this Jordan, but now I have become two camps. Save me, I pray, from the hand of my brother Esau, for I am afraid he will come and attack me, and also the mothers with their children. But you have said, "I will surely make you prosper and will make your descendants like the sand of the sea, which cannot be counted."'...

Jacob looked up and there was Esau, coming with his four hundred men; so he divided the children among Leah, Rachel and the two female servants. He put the female servants and their children in front, Leah and her children next, and Rachel and Joseph in the rear. He himself went on ahead and bowed down to the ground seven times as he approached his brother.

But Esau ran to meet Jacob and embraced him; he threw his arms around his neck and kissed him. And they wept.

GENESIS 32:9–12; 33:1–4

When I saw her, I burst into tears. I was weary, for the flight had been long and I was laden with luggage and my young children. To my delight, not only were my parents waiting for me at baggage claim, but my sister had flown in as well.

'You came!' I said.

'Yes, I found a cheap flight and thought it would be fun to surprise you.'

Surprise me she did. The week was an unexpected gift, for not only were we given a lovely beachside apartment to enjoy, but I had three family members with me whom I don't get to see often or share my children with. Our reunion was tearful in a good way.

Going back a few millennia, Jacob isn't sure how his meeting with his brother will turn out. As we saw yesterday, Jacob is right to be concerned, for he had to flee from Esau or be killed. Now that 20 years have passed since his deception of Esau, Jacob hears from the Lord that it is time to return to Canaan. He plots and prepares for the meeting, seeking ways to soften Esau's reaction, such as sending along gifts of livestock. Then the night before they meet, Jacob experiences an unexpected encounter with the Lord, in which he wrestles with God, finally coming to the end of himself and his self-sufficiency. He receives a new name, Israel, signifying a change in character. No longer will he be known as someone who deceives. (The full story can be found in Genesis 32—33.)

So it's a different man who meets with Esau the next day, and amazingly we witness a joyful, tearful reunion. Jacob bows down to Esau, humbling himself before him, signifying that he no longer lords the stolen birthright and blessings over him. In a move filled with grace, Esau responds with an embrace, and though wrongs have been committed in the past, forgiveness is extended as the two are reconciled.

As I read the story, I think of King David's song to the Lord in which he says, 'How good and pleasant it is when God's people live together in unity!' (Psalm 133:1). Indeed, how good it is for Esau and Jacob to be reconciled, and for Jacob to submit to the Lord, acknowledging that God is God and he is not.

When we read this story, we might do so with a heavy heart, being mired in conflict with our siblings or those who are as close as a sister or brother. We might lack the hope that healing and reconciliation can occur in our situation. But we can ask God to give us the gift of faith, that we might pray for him to work a miracle in our lives, bringing peace and love to those who have been estranged. It may take some time, humility and maybe even the showering of gifts, as we see in the case of Jacob and Esau, but the Lord has a full stock of resources for us to access as we usher in his kingdom.

If you're feeling trapped or hopeless, may the Lord give you the gift of hope today, and may he work through you as an agent of peace, love and change.

## Prayer

*Lord God, Jacob received a new name when finally he fell down before you. No longer would he be known as a deceiver, but as someone who wrestled with you. I rejoice that peace came to that family as he and Esau abandoned their fight. And so before you I set the situations I'm concerned about, asking that you would work your freeing power. I think of warring factions among nations that have roots going down through the generations; Lord, have mercy. For those issues closer to home, which might cut to the heart and tie me up inside, Christ, have mercy. Thank you, Father God, that you are the Lord who makes all things new, and that you have the power to bring change and hope. Please bring about more tearful reunions of the good sort.*

# Tuesday

# A dreamer in an ornate coat

Now Israel loved Joseph more than any of his other sons, because he had been born to him in his old age; and he made an ornate robe for him. When his brothers saw that their father loved him more than any of them, they hated him and could not speak a kind word to him...

Now his brothers had gone to graze their father's flocks near Shechem, and Israel said to Joseph, 'As you know, your brothers are grazing the flocks near Shechem. Come, I am going to send you to them.'

'Very well,' he replied.

So he said to him, 'Go and see if all is well with your brothers and with the flocks, and bring word back to me.' Then he sent him off from the Valley of Hebron.

When Joseph arrived at Shechem, a man found him wandering around in the fields and asked him, 'What are you looking for?'

He replied, 'I'm looking for my brothers. Can you tell me where they are grazing their flocks?'

'They have moved on from here,' the man answered. 'I heard them say, "Let's go to Dothan."'

So Joseph went after his brothers and found them near Dothan. But they saw him in the distance, and before he reached them, they plotted to kill him.

'Here comes that dreamer!' they said to each other. 'Come now, let's kill him and throw him into one of these cisterns and say that a ferocious animal devoured him. Then we'll see what comes of his dreams.'

GENESIS 37:3–4, 12–20

When mind-numbingly awful things happen, we can find it difficult to understand why, or to believe that God can redeem the situation. A daughter dies in a car accident. Persecuted people flee their homes in search of safety. A brother turns on a brother, betraying him and cutting all ties. This side of heaven, we may never find the full answer of why God allows heart-wrenching incidents to happen, but we can believe that he will work to redeem them.

We see God's redemptive power at work in the life of Joseph, Israel's favourite son. If we read Genesis 37 as background, we see that Joseph was unwise to share his dreams with his family members—especially the dreams which placed him above his brothers and parents (Genesis 37:5–11). Sibling rivalry seems rife in Old Testament stories, intensified when parents harbour favourites. Already the stage is set for a confrontation.

Israel asks Joseph to find his brothers and he obeys, setting off on a journey that probably takes him four or five days. He gets lost, however, and is found 'wandering around in the fields'. Maybe he's weary, or perhaps, as one called a dreamer, he becomes absorbed in his thoughts and loses track of where he is going. A man finds him in the fields, which was probably seen as providential by the original readers. If Joseph hadn't come across this man, who directed him to where his brothers were, he may have returned to his father unharmed. But in reaching them, he suffers at their hands. The Lord allows Joseph to be wrenched from his family, in time redeeming the sins of the brothers in his greater plan of salvation, as we will see tomorrow.[7]

In our lives, however, we aren't often given this divine objectivity and we don't know how our stories will end. Therefore we can struggle to understand why the Lord allows atrocities, disease and hardships to occur. As we live in a fallen world, bad things will always happen—and although the Lord can redeem them, I don't believe he causes the evil to happen. Nor does the Lord delight in our sorrows, for he would have us thrive and flourish and experience his joy. Yet sometimes things happen to us that God can use later for his glory and our good, as he does in Joseph's story.

As you consider the dreamer stripped of his ornate coat, think about the confusion and pain he must have felt while sitting in the cistern (37:23–24), left to die while wondering if his dreams will also perish. As he cries out to the Lord in his uncertainty and bewilderment, I believe he understands that the Lord hasn't abandoned him, which is my prayer for us today.

## Prayer

*Lord God, at times I may have flaunted my specialness, like Joseph. At times I may feel I've been thrown into a smelly sewer, left to rot. But you love and cherish me. You will never leave or reject me, and although things happen that I can't comprehend, I know that you can turn these things to good. They may sting and pierce me inside, but you can redeem them. Please bring good out of the horrific situations I witness in the world—and more so, please intervene, that good may triumph over evil to the praise and glory of your name. Help me to bring light and hope to those whom I meet.*

# Wednesday

# Good from evil

When Joseph's brothers saw that their father was dead, they said, 'What if Joseph holds a grudge against us and pays us back for all the wrongs we did to him?' So they sent word to Joseph, saying, 'Your father left these instructions before he died: "This is what you are to say to Joseph: I ask you to forgive your brothers the sins and the wrongs they committed in treating you so badly." Now please forgive the sins of the servants of the God of your father.' When their message came to him, Joseph wept.

His brothers then came and threw themselves down before him. 'We are your slaves,' they said.

But Joseph said to them, 'Don't be afraid. Am I in the place of God? You intended to harm me, but God intended it for good to accomplish what is now being done, the saving of many lives. So then, don't be afraid. I will provide for you and your children.' And he reassured them and spoke kindly to them.
GENESIS 50:15–21

'Revenge imprisons us; forgiveness sets us free.'[8] So writes Robin Oake in *Father, Forgive* when he recounts the story of how, in a press conference shortly after his son was killed, he extended forgiveness to his son's murderer. The media were incredulous that a man could forgive someone they termed a terrorist, and although Robin shares how his tears came close to overwhelming him, he also points to a strength of will to forgive that he saw as a gift from the Lord. For this father, forgiveness would impart freedom from bitterness.

Another life freed from resentment is that of Joseph. So much has happened since we saw him abandoned and sold for the price of a slave. After many years and hardships, he rose to prominence as

Pharaoh's second-in-command, in charge of all of Egypt. Yet he never forgot his father and brothers, longing for them. When famine hit the land, with Joseph prepared for it through having interpreted Pharaoh's dreams, his brothers came to Egypt wanting to buy grain. They didn't realise they were approaching their brother, whom they must have assumed was long dead. But Joseph knew, and had mercy on them. He finally revealed himself with great emotion, embracing them and welcoming them to come and live with him (see Genesis 45:1–7). Jacob enjoyed the pleasure of being reunited with his beloved son and embracing and blessing his grandchildren.

But after Jacob dies, the brothers start to fear for their lives, as Joseph could call for their ruin. Claiming the protection of their father, they ask Joseph to forgive their wrongdoing. We see the mature and grace-filled Joseph respond with open arms as they humble themselves before him. He assures them of his continued care and provision.

Note, however, that although Joseph extends forgiveness in deed, he doesn't do so through his words, saying instead (my paraphrase), 'Who am I to forgive you? Am I God?' We see again that in the Old Testament, person-to-person forgiveness is rare, for the all-powerful Lord is the one who grants pardon. Joseph is not the source of forgiveness but God's agent of it as he extends grace and love to his family.

Joseph also acknowledges the Lord's redemptive action throughout his life (which we looked at yesterday) when he says, 'God intended it for good' (v. 20). If Joseph hadn't been thrown into that cistern, and if he hadn't spent all those years in jail, he wouldn't have risen to prominence in Pharaoh's household at the opportune moment with the influence to save his family and many others. As he surveys the past he sees God's hand in bringing forth good from evil.

May we too be granted this sense of objectivity when we look back over our lives, with its twists and turns and what might seem to be trails going off into the wilderness. He who brought forth good in the life of Joseph's family can do so in ours too.

## Prayer

*Lord God, you know that I fail, and that I suffer not only from my own wrongdoing but from that of others, living as we do in a world that is not as you created it. I need your grace and mercy; I long for your peace and healing in a fractured world. May I be an agent of change as I pass along the gifts from your abundance, whether those unseen such as love, peace, grace or joy, or material goods such as the grain that Joseph provided for his family. May these gifts bring forth softened and receptive hearts and renewed relationships.*

## Thursday

# Rescue plan

Now Moses was tending the flock of Jethro his father-in-law, the priest of Midian, and he led the flock to the far side of the wilderness and came to Horeb, the mountain of God. There the angel of the Lord appeared to him in flames of fire from within a bush. Moses saw that though the bush was on fire it did not burn up. So Moses thought, 'I will go over and see this strange sight—why the bush does not burn up.'

When the Lord saw that he had gone over to look, God called to him from within the bush, 'Moses! Moses!'

And Moses said, 'Here I am.'

'Do not come any closer,' God said. 'Take off your sandals, for the place where you are standing is holy ground.' Then he said, 'I am the God of your father, the God of Abraham, the God of Isaac and the God of Jacob.' At this, Moses hid his face, because he was afraid to look at God.

The Lord said, 'I have indeed seen the misery of my people in Egypt. I have heard them crying out because of their slave drivers, and I am concerned about their suffering. So I have come down to rescue them from the hand of the Egyptians and to bring them up out of that land into a good and spacious land, a land flowing with milk and honey—the home of the Canaanites, Hittites, Amorites, Perizzites, Hivites and Jebusites... So now, go. I am sending you to Pharaoh to bring my people the Israelites out of Egypt.'

EXODUS 3:1–8, 10

Charles Colson fell from his position of power with an almighty crash. Arrested for obstructing justice during the Watergate scandal, he was given a copy of C.S. Lewis' *Mere Christianity*, which, in the light of his personal crisis, he read with interest. He committed his life to Christ after reading it, and although he served time in prison for his crimes, he turned his life around. Out of a promise not to forget those in prison, he created Prison Fellowship, an international organisation that serves prisoners in the name of Christ. Before he died in 2012 he was honoured with several prestigious awards for his positive influence on society. He was a changed man.

Moses was a murderer, but he became one of the great leaders of God's people. Exodus 2 tells how Moses killed an Egyptian who was mistreating a Hebrew, one of his own people. The text doesn't say if Moses knew that he himself was a Hebrew; nor do we know what motivated him to intervene, and then to hide the body. But when Pharaoh found out, Moses could no longer claim any rights as an adopted son but had to flee for his life. He went to Midian, where he found a wife and made his home.

After 40 years of living as a foreigner, content with a quiet life, Moses' world changes in an instant when the Lord appears to him in a burning bush. Though he has taken the life of an Egyptian, the Lord forgives him, choosing him as the one to deliver his people from their oppression in Egypt. This man who once took unwise action in the face of injustice will now stand against the slavery of his people.

The road will be hard, and the people and even Moses himself will run from his leadership, but through the oppression and trials he will grow in confidence and stature. He who stammers will eventually become a man whom the people listen to and follow. But first he has to accept God's seemingly impossible commission to release his people from Pharaoh.

We can find encouragement from the story of Moses, for he is such a fallible leader—prone to questioning God and having his brother speak in his place—and yet the Lord uses him as his instrument. Moses' growth and emergence as one of the great fathers of the faith takes decades as, trial by trial, he gains confidence in the Lord and in himself. And I believe that letting go of his identity as an escaped murderer forms an important part of his acceptance of God's commission to lead the people out of slavery.

We may face completely different challenges from those that Moses encountered, but we can find hope and strength in our identity as those who are forgiven through the death of Jesus on the cross. There we can deposit our lack of confidence and fear; there we can ask God to relieve us of our wrongdoing; and there we will receive our commissions, unique as each of us is. There will the Lord bestow on us his compassion, grace and love. May we know his still, small voice, that we may sense the next step in our commission as his ambassadors of love and truth.

## Prayer

*Father God, the years go by and I don't always understand how you are at work. I'm sorry for the way I doubt you; I grieve the way I fail you. I see Moses with all of his shortcomings and sins and marvel that you made him into a great and mighty leader, and that gives me hope. Make me into your pliable instrument, that I might work with you to usher in your kingdom here on earth. Please be the advocate for the weak and those who are sinned against, and help me to stand up in holy, godly ways against injustice. Give me courage and strength, and put me in the best place to make a difference according to your wisdom.*

# Friday

# True advocacy

Then the Lord said to Moses, 'Go down, because your people, whom you brought up out of Egypt, have become corrupt. They have been quick to turn away from what I commanded them and have made themselves an idol cast in the shape of a calf. They have bowed down to it and sacrificed to it and have said, "These are your gods, Israel, who brought you up out of Egypt."

'I have seen these people,' the Lord said to Moses, 'and they are a stiff-necked people. Now leave me alone so that my anger may burn against them and that I may destroy them. Then I will make you into a great nation.'

But Moses sought the favour of the Lord his God. 'Lord,' he said, 'why should your anger burn against your people, whom you brought out of Egypt with great power and a mighty hand? Why should the Egyptians say, "It was with evil intent that he brought them out, to kill them in the mountains and to wipe them off the face of the earth"? Turn from your fierce anger; relent and do not bring disaster on your people...' Then the Lord relented and did not bring on his people the disaster he had threatened.

EXODUS 32:7–12, 14

Walking on the streets of London, I often see people hunched over, gazing at their smartphones. I too can be one of those people as I check social media sites and my inbox, but I am conscious of the pull of these devices and I try to work hard not to let them become an idol in my life. They can provide the means to information, community and belonging, so in writing about the danger that they might become idols, I don't want to suggest that they are all negative. Rather that because we human beings were created to worship, these devices can become addictive if we're not careful. They can disrupt our relationships with others and with God—as Moses found that the Israelites could be just as easily distracted as we are.

Many people see similarities between Moses and Jesus. There are differences, of course, as Jesus is the Son of God and Moses a mere man, but a key role that they both play is to act as advocates on behalf of God's people. As we see in 1 John 2:1, Jesus is called our advocate with the Father through his ultimate sacrifice on the cross, which bestows freedom on us. And as we see in the story about the golden calf, Moses pleads with the Lord for his people.

While Moses is with the Lord up the mountain, the people get bored and distracted. Even though the Lord has released them from slavery in Egypt by sending plague after plague and, finally, causing the miraculous parting of the Red Sea, they forget what he has done for them. Tired of waiting, and encouraged by Moses' brother Aaron, they quickly change their allegiance by melting gold and fashioning it into a calf that they will worship. The Lord's anger burns against them, and he threatens to blot them out from the face of the earth. But Moses asks the Lord to relent, pointing out that it wouldn't be a good witness to the Egyptians if he were to obliterate his people. The Lord turns away his anger, and Moses leaves the Lord's presence to sort things out at the bottom of the mountain.

When Moses sees the extent of the people's sins, he rages against them, smashing the tablets of the commandments to signify an end to the covenant relationship. Only after a winnowing of the people, with about 3000 people dying, does Moses return to the Lord to plead forgiveness for them (Exodus 32:27–32). Although the Lord doesn't relent fully at this point, he promises to punish the wrongdoers only.

Moses' advocacy results in the Lord not wiping out his people. Indeed, Moses stands in the breach to keep Israel from destruction, as the psalmist later says in Psalm 106, which recounts God's mercy in the midst of the unfaithfulness of his people. In verse 23 the psalmist names Moses as God's 'chosen one' who prevented the Lord's 'wrath from destroying them' and kept the faith, welcoming from a distance the Saviour of his people (see Hebrews 11:24–28).

That advocate, Jesus, intercedes for us even now before his Father, as Paul says in his letter to the Romans (8:34). His work on the cross acts as a glue that binds together God's covenant, and no longer do we need to fear the Lord's wrath. The one who stands in our place releases us from the consequences of our sins. As forgiven people, may we not worship any false gods—whether of gold or of success, relationships, influence or our electronic devices—but only the true and living Lord.

## Prayer

*Lord Jesus, you speak on my behalf before the great judge. I would cower and tremble, but I know that your love frees me from this fear. May I live in confidence in you and your work in my life. Thank you that you live in me through the dwelling of your Holy Spirit, and that you empower me to stand tall in my identity as your child. May I advocate for those who cannot speak for themselves, whether those shunned from their countries or those languishing on the streets, without homes. I long to put my faith into practice, loving Lord, that I may share your goodness with those in my local community and around the world, for your praise and glory.*

# Saturday

# Radiant faces

The Lord said to Moses, 'Chisel out two stone tablets like the first ones, and I will write on them the words that were on the first tablets, which you broke... So Moses chiselled out two stone tablets like the first ones and went up Mount Sinai early in the morning, as the Lord had commanded him; and he carried the two stone tablets in his hands. Then the Lord came down in the cloud and stood there with him and proclaimed his name, the Lord. And he passed in front of Moses, proclaiming, 'The Lord, the Lord, the compassionate and gracious God, slow to anger, abounding in love and faithfulness, maintaining love to thousands, and forgiving wickedness, rebellion and sin. Yet he does not leave the guilty unpunished; he punishes the children and their children for the sin of the parents to the third and fourth generation.'

Moses bowed to the ground at once and worshipped. 'Lord,' he said, 'if I have found favour in your eyes, then let the Lord go with us. Although this is a stiff-necked people, forgive our wickedness and our sin, and take us as your inheritance.'

Then the Lord said: 'I am making a covenant with you. Before all your people I will do wonders never before done in any nation in all the world. The people you live among will see how awesome is the work that I, the Lord, will do for you. Obey what I command you today.'

EXODUS 34:1, 4–11

Some Christians shy away from reading the Old Testament, thinking that the Lord portrayed there is one of judgement and wrath. But as we see in our readings, the Lord in the Pentateuch (the first five books of the Bible) is a forgiving God, extending grace and mercy to his errant people. Though he says he will eradicate the Israelites, he doesn't do it, for he hears the cries of leaders such as Abraham, who negotiated with him (Genesis 18:22–32), and Moses, as we saw yesterday.

After the incident in which the Israelites prostitute themselves to the golden calf, the Lord again shows mercy on his people as he reveals his glory to Moses. Calling for another set of tablets to replace the ones Moses destroyed in anger, the Lord promises to renew his covenant with his people. First, however, in a holy act—so holy that only Moses can witness it—he proclaims his name to Moses, defining his identity as one who is compassionate, 'slow to anger, abounding in love and faithfulness, maintaining love to thousands, and forgiving wickedness, rebellion and sin' (vv. 6–7). Moses responds by falling to the ground to worship.

When we consider the attributes of the Lord, do we respond as Moses did? We have the privilege of intimacy with God through Jesus and the Holy Spirit, but with this closeness we can be tempted to forget or downplay the gravitas and holiness of the living Lord. He who forgives wickedness and rebellion longs that we would grow more like him, abhorring sin and not requiring so much forgiveness. He yearns that we would grow in holiness as we walk with him day by day.

Moses had the pleasure of spending 40 days on the mountain with the Lord, and the people had to wait for him to return. Moses couldn't help but be touched by God's glory, so much that his face radiated light and love (Exodus 34:29). We too can exude the joy of the Lord as we ask the Holy Spirit to dwell within us. As we meditate on his love and faithfulness, we are led to worship, receiving his peace, affirmation and radiance. We, like Moses, reflect his glory.

## Prayer

*Holy God, I bow down before you and worship you, for you created me and you define holiness. Search me, O Lord, and reveal any of my hidden sins, that I might confess them to you at the cross and be free of them. Create in me a pure heart, O God, and give me steadfastness and tenacity to love and serve you with my whole being. May I, while naming any sins of the previous days or weeks to you, know your loving compassion and mercy as I receive your forgiveness. And may I pass along your love and forgiveness to those who have wronged me, for I want to forgive as I've been forgiven.*

# Spiritual exercises and questions for individual reflection and group discussion

## The living cross

You will need two pieces of wood or two sticks to form a cross, fixed with a small nail, or a ready-made cross; paper; tape or adhesive putty.

When you think of the cross, what words come to mind? In this exercise, we will consider the cross as alive—an active agent for change as it brings us freedom from specific sins, such as the bitterness that lingers after a betrayal or the anger that festers after being wronged.

If you are able, construct a cross out of wood or sticks, or use a ready-made cross. As you hold the cross, quieten yourself before God and ask his Holy Spirit to reveal to you a specific memory, person or conversation that causes you anger, bitterness or hurt. Write on the paper anything that you'd like to release to the Lord, asking for forgiveness if necessary.

With some tape or adhesive putty, stick the paper to the cross, asking God through his Holy Spirit to bring forgiveness for your part in, or your response to, the situation or person. As you wait before the Lord, ask him to fill you with peace, joy, love and release. You may be tempted to shorten this part of the exercise, but stay in the silence if you can, for the Lord through his still, small voice may impart to you healing words of love.

I've put this exercise first, for you can repeat it throughout Lent as a key way of enacting confession and receiving forgiveness.

## Fashioning a crown of thorns

> You will need a polystyrene wreath; toothpicks; flowers for Easter Day.

An activity you may want to undertake throughout Lent, which works well for adults and children, is to make a crown of thorns. Place the polystyrene wreath on the table where you eat, with the toothpicks nearby. Each day, each person at the table (if you share your meals with others) takes a toothpick and places it into the wreath while confessing a sin that they committed that day. Depending on those present, the sin can be spoken aloud or internally. On Easter morning, replace the toothpicks with flowers to signify Christ's healing sacrifice for our sins.[9]

## Releasing and loving our siblings

We're going to think about sibling relationships in this exercise, inspired by the readings on Cain and Abel, Jacob and Esau, and Joseph and his brothers. If you are an only child, perhaps you can think about cousins or close friends who have been like sisters or brothers to you. You can also pray for any children, godchildren or grandchildren you may have and their relationships with each other.

Approach the Lord in prayer, asking him to bring before your mind's eye a family member to whom you need to be reconciled. (Of course, you might be living in harmony with your family. If this is the case, spend time giving thanks and praying for your relations.)

If God's Holy Spirit reveals to you a person or a situation, consider writing them a letter that you probably won't and shouldn't send. In it, confess how you've sinned against them, naming the specifics as they come to your mind. Ask God to help you extend forgiveness to the person for the way they have sinned against you. Then shred or destroy the letter and ask God to make these sins unreadable. Pray that God would restore and strengthen your relationship, that you might be free to love each other.

If you're able, write a letter, text or email that you will send to the person. In it include words of blessing and affirmation as appropriate, saying that you have been thinking of them and that you wish them well.

## Dissolving deception

You will need a bowl of water; some table salt.

Sometimes we deceive others; sometimes we deceive ourselves. Quieten yourself before the triune God, thanking him that he never leaves you. Consider Abram and how, motivated by hunger and fear, he relied on his own judgements instead of looking to God. Is hunger or fear driving you? Ask God to show you any places of deception lurking in your soul.

As you ask the Lord to dissolve your hunger, fear or deception, pour the salt into the water and watch it dissolve, believing that the Lord dissipates your sins. Ask him for his presence and love to fill any empty places in your heart, mind and soul, that you might feel his pleasure.[10]

## Questions for reflection and discussion

- How do you imagine the world might be if Adam and Eve hadn't eaten the forbidden fruit?
- We've seen so much sibling strife and rivalry in our readings for these first days of Lent. What insights have you gained from engaging with these readings? Why do you think forgiveness within one's family can be so difficult?
- Are you surprised that Jacob got away with his crime of stealing Esau's birthright? How did he suffer for his sin? How was he restored?

- In thinking about Abraham and Sarah, consider what things you've had to wait for. What did you learn in the process of waiting, and how did God change you? Was it worth the wait?
- We saw the Lord change Jacob's name to Israel, a practice which we'll come across again in our readings. What was the significance of the change in name? What do you see as your true name?
- The grand story of Joseph gives us hope as we see how the Lord redeemed his suffering and used him as an instrument of mercy. But Joseph must have wondered what was going on when he was languishing in the cistern or in prison. How do you think he kept on keeping faith in God? How have you fostered faith when you've faced situations of strife or hardship?
- In anger, Moses smashed the tablets containing the law of the Lord when he saw how the people had turned to false gods. To what extent do you see Moses' anger as righteous anger? For us, how can we foster holiness and a healthy fear of the Lord without resorting to anger and sin?

# Week 2

# Flawed but Forgiven Kings

This week, we turn to the period of time when God's people yearn to be like the other nations who have a king over them. The prophet Samuel eventually relents and appoints Saul as the first king—with dire consequences, as we shall see. Even King David, whom the Lord calls 'a man after my own heart' (1 Samuel 13:14), is flawed and in need of forgiveness and restoration—which we find at the living cross.

We move briefly to God's people at the time of the exile, when Ezra and Nehemiah call for a time of national repentance. We too can gather communally to confess the sins of our nations, asking for forgiveness and peace.

We end the week with a look at the Psalms and Proverbs, songs of love and lament and words of wisdom. Both of our selections show our need for forgiveness and how God redeems us from our wrongdoing.

# Sunday

# Wholehearted return

The ark remained at Kiriath Jearim a long time—twenty years in all.

Then all the people of Israel turned back to the Lord. So Samuel said to all the Israelites, 'If you are returning to the Lord with all your hearts, then rid yourselves of the foreign gods and the Ashtoreths and commit yourselves to the Lord and serve him only, and he will deliver you out of the hand of the Philistines.' So the Israelites put away their Baals and Ashtoreths, and served the Lord only.

Then Samuel said, 'Assemble all Israel at Mizpah, and I will intercede with the Lord for you.' When they had assembled at Mizpah, they drew water and poured it out before the Lord. On that day they fasted and there they confessed, 'We have sinned against the Lord.'

1 SAMUEL 7:2–6

Half-heartedness seems rampant today, with people resisting commitment not only to church but to other community groups. But recently I heard a heart-warming story from a church leader who was leading a course to introduce people to the Christian faith. At the end of the six weeks, a man came up to him and said, 'I said at the beginning that I wouldn't change while I was on this course, but I have moved closer towards God. And what strikes me is how your faith in God is the single most important thing in your life.' The leader was humbled and thrilled that this man had noticed how much his faith meant to him and how wholehearted he was in his pursuit of it.

As the Israelites settled into the promised land under Joshua's leadership, they were given victories against their enemies as they enjoyed the favour of the Lord. But as the years passed, they struggled to stay pure before the Lord and to keep his commandments. One continual temptation was to break the law given in Deuteronomy 7:1–4, which instructed them not to intermarry with the local people, 'for they will turn your children away from following me to serve other gods' (v. 4). With the introduction of foreign spouses, they started to worship the foreign gods and stray from their commitment to purity and holiness.

During this time of turning away from the Lord, Samuel was born as one set apart. Early in his life in the temple, he learned to discern and hear the voice of the Lord; he needed to mature in this practice so that he would be ready for the time when, as a prophet, he would pass the Lord's message to his people. Though the Israelites wanted him to crown a king over them, he resisted, but eventually he acquiesced and anointed their first king, Saul.

In the passage we're exploring today, Samuel seizes the moment as the people soften their hearts towards the Lord. To bring about a real change of behaviour, however, they need to repent with their whole heart—no half measures. That will include ridding themselves of all foreign gods, an act that could upset many homes that were committed to a mixture of deities. In the Hebrew, the word for 'rid yourselves' (v. 3) implies putting something away, never to pick it up again.[11]

Repentance includes not only turning from, but turning to, as we see in the next phrase of Samuel's exhortation to the people: 'commit yourselves to the Lord'. Here the Hebrew means fixing or establishing one's heart permanently on to something, which in this case means holding on tightly to the Lord and his ways.[12]

The third part of Samuel's command, 'serve him only', implies an important distinguishing feature for the Israelites.[13] They are to put away all idol worship and return to the Lord as the only true and living God. Their hearts will remain pure and committed only if they relinquish the hold that other gods have on them.

May we also shed our attachment to other loves and return to the Lord, the one who loves us unceasingly and with abandon.

## Prayer

*God of our ancestors, help me to learn from those who have gone before me in the faith, that I might avoid their failings. I'm sorry for the ways in which I haven't followed you, and I want to commit to you with my whole heart, soul, mind and body—all that I have and all that I am. Prick my ears and conscience this day, that I might sense your loving call to return. Help me to hear you and to discern your voice, that I might obey your gentle or firm commands. I want to be transformed into your likeness, that I can share your grace and truth with a hurting world.*

# Monday

# A monument to self

Samuel said to Saul, 'I am the one the Lord sent to anoint you king over his people Israel; so listen now to the message from the Lord. This is what the Lord Almighty says: "I will punish the Amalekites for what they did to Israel when they waylaid them as they came up from Egypt. Now go, attack the Amalekites and totally destroy all that belongs to them. Do not spare them; put to death men and women, children and infants, cattle and sheep, camels and donkeys."'…

Then Saul attacked the Amalekites all the way from Havilah to Shur, near the eastern border of Egypt. He took Agag king of the Amalekites alive, and all his people he totally destroyed with the sword. But Saul and the army spared Agag and the best of the sheep and cattle, the fat calves and lambs—everything that was good. These they were unwilling to destroy completely, but everything that was despised and weak they totally destroyed.

Then the word of the Lord came to Samuel: 'I regret that I have made Saul king, because he has turned away from me and has not carried out my instructions.' Samuel was angry, and he cried out to the Lord all that night.

Early in the morning Samuel got up and went to meet Saul, but he was told, 'Saul has gone to Carmel. There he has set up a monument in his own honour and has turned and gone on down to Gilgal.'

1 SAMUEL 15:1–3, 7–12

Those who love and care for children can tell when a child is only sorry that they've been caught, and not sorry for the deed they have committed. A glare, attitude or curling of the lip indicates that they don't actually want to repent but are being made to do so. But after discussion, fervent silent prayer and perhaps a punishment, the parent or carer may witness the child experiencing true sorrow—much to the parent's relief.

This is not so, however, in the case of Saul, Israel's first king. He doesn't obey the Lord's instructions to destroy the Amalekites completely, and as we read further in 1 Samuel 15, when Samuel challenges him, he blames others and finds excuses for not killing the king and for keeping back the best of the livestock. In his cheery greeting to Samuel (v. 13), he either tries to deceive the prophet with his 'Job done', or appears deluded.

Saul hoards the best of the plunder for his own means and, far from worshipping the Lord, sets up a monument praising himself. Later, we see that when he says he has sinned, he appears to be paying lip service to Samuel. He, like the unrepentant child, is sorry only that he's been caught. A true turning back to the Lord never occurs, which is confirmed in 1 Samuel 19:9–10 when Saul tries to kill God's choice of the next king, David.

Then the Lord regrets that he appointed Saul as king.[14]

We can't force children—or spouses, family members or friends—to repent. Nor does the Lord make Saul turn from his self-centred and evil ways, for God always respects an individual's freedom to choose their own actions. We can, however, pray tenaciously that the Lord's Holy Spirit would soften and loosen any hard-heartedness in our loved ones and opponents, bringing reconciliation and renewal. And, of course, we need to attend to our own motives, pride and actions, asking God to show us where we are at fault—the log in our own eye versus the splinter in our neighbour's (Matthew 7:3–5).

Today, why not pray for any situations of conflict that you know of, that the Lord may bring restoration and peace?

## Prayer

*Lord God, so often I'm stubborn, digging in my heels when others point out my failures and faults. I don't like to be wrong, and I don't like to repent. Help me to bend my will to you, that I might serve and love you and others. I want to be your vessel, and I know that when I'm concerned only for my own agenda, I miss out on opportunities to reach out to others. Love the world through me, I pray, as you widen my horizons and imagination. May I share your light and love far and wide.*

# Tuesday

# Disaster at the door

When Abigail saw David, she quickly got off her donkey and bowed down before David with her face to the ground. She fell at his feet and said: 'Pardon your servant, my lord, and let me speak to you; hear what your servant has to say. Please pay no attention, my lord, to that wicked man Nabal. He is just like his name—his name means Fool, and folly goes with him. And as for me, your servant, I did not see the men my lord sent...

'Please forgive your servant's presumption. The Lord your God will certainly make a lasting dynasty for my lord, because you fight the Lord's battles, and no wrongdoing will be found in you as long as you live... When the Lord has fulfilled for my lord every good thing he promised concerning him and has appointed him ruler over Israel, my lord will not have on his conscience the staggering burden of needless bloodshed or of having avenged himself. And when the Lord your God has brought my lord success, remember your servant.'

David said to Abigail, 'Praise be to the Lord, the God of Israel, who has sent you today to meet me. May you be blessed for your good judgement and for keeping me from bloodshed this day and from avenging myself with my own hands.'

1 SAMUEL 25:23–25, 28, 30–33

Abigail is a popular name for Christians to give their daughter, not only because it means 'father's joy' but because the Bible calls this character in 1 Samuel 'intelligent and beautiful' (25:3), with her actions bearing out the description. Not so flattering is the name Nabal, meaning 'fool', an apt moniker for the surly and inhospitable man depicted here. It may be that the narrator gave this nickname to him or that he became what he was named.

Abigail acts quickly to avert disaster for David. When he and his men were rebuffed by Nabal, not shown the traditional hospitality in return for the protection they had provided for Nabal's animals, David immediately turned to the sword in vengeance (vv. 7–13). Abigail, however, knows that David is a future king, something he seems to have forgotten. She points out how damaging a mass slaughter would be for his reputation. Perhaps she also senses how hungry the army must have been, and how David's stomach may have been driving him into a rash decision. After she arranges a generous gift of food for him and his men (v. 18), David, appeased, relents.

Abigail then chooses the right time to tell her foolish husband that she has saved his skin—not the same night, when he's partying and drunk, but the next day, when the wine has drained out of him. His life-force drains away too, and ten days later he dies, leaving Abigail free for David to ask her to marry him. Although she is one of several wives, she will be an asset to him in wisdom and beauty.

Her act in seeking pardon may be calculated and made on behalf of another, but it proves a wise and humble way to promote peace and accord. David also shows that he has the strength of character to change his mind when he's wrong: he doesn't have to dig in his heels in an immovable stance. The future king has a pliable heart, willing to take counsel from someone who at that time would not have been seen as his equal.

We can take heart from this story—not only about the life-giving nature of forgiveness but also about the way a humble person can avert disaster on behalf of another, whether a spouse, family member, colleague or close friend. Standing up for what is good and right, with grace and winsomeness, can bring about an ending far different from the one that may have happened otherwise.

## Prayer

*Triune God, you have bequeathed me your wisdom and grace, for I am made in your likeness. May I embody truth with grace, and may I approach tricky situations not with a defensive spirit but with humility and a generous nature. May your Spirit in me work to promote the healing of relationships and peace. I boldly ask that international disasters might be averted through the kind of grace that Abigail showed to David, that when leaders meet, trust might be established and amicable agreements reached. I long for your peace to reign on this earth as it does in heaven.*

# Wednesday

# Cover-up

Then Nathan said to David, 'You are the man! This is what the Lord, the God of Israel, says: "I anointed you king over Israel, and I delivered you from the hand of Saul. I gave your master's house to you, and your master's wives into your arms. I gave you all Israel and Judah. And if all this had been too little, I would have given you even more. Why did you despise the word of the Lord by doing what is evil in his eyes? You struck down Uriah the Hittite with the sword and took his wife to be your own. You killed him with the sword of the Ammonites. Now, therefore, the sword shall never depart from your house, because you despised me and took the wife of Uriah the Hittite to be your own."

'This is what the Lord says: "Out of your own household I am going to bring calamity on you. Before your very eyes I will take your wives and give them to one who is close to you, and he will sleep with your wives in broad daylight. You did it in secret, but I will do this thing in broad daylight before all Israel."'

Then David said to Nathan, 'I have sinned against the Lord.'

Nathan replied, 'The Lord has taken away your sin. You are not going to die. But because by doing this you have shown utter contempt for the Lord, the son born to you will die.'

2 SAMUEL 12:7–14

The word of the Lord comes to David through the prophet Nathan, blasting away David's lies and cover-up job. Though David may have thought that he had sorted out his sin (he had slept with his soldier's wife while lounging at home, when he should have been away at war), he can hide no longer. His wrongful deeds, the punishment for which should have been death for both him and Bathsheba, have been exposed.

The ideal king has fallen from grace by his act, which led to another sinful act, and another. The Hittite soldier—upstanding, though a foreigner—refused to sleep with his now-pregnant wife when David beckoned him back from battle, so David had him killed. Adultery turned to murder and the cover-up spiralled out of control, with David's power as king hoodwinking him into thinking that he could get away with his crimes. But unlike neighbouring kings, who may have escaped punishment even if discovered, David serves a higher God—the Lord. The Holy One of Israel stops David in his tracks.

Nathan delivers the verdict: David will live, but no longer will he enjoy easy victories. Now, as the Lord tells him, he'll have to face strife and enmity from within his own family. And the child he and Bathsheba have conceived will die—a consequence of, if not the punishment for, his sin.[15] His wrongful actions have a ripple effect on his and his family's life and the life of the kingdom.

Yet David shows himself still to be the ideal king, for unlike Saul, who evaded repentance until a half-hearted stab at it was his last option, David confesses his sin immediately, naming him whom he has spurned: 'I have sinned against the Lord' (v. 13). He makes no excuses and blames no one else; he knows he is at fault. His heart is open to correction; he repents and petitions the Lord on behalf of his young child through fasting and prayer.

Although the story (well worth reading from 2 Samuel 11) reads like a horrifying modern account of lies, subterfuge, murder and deceit, all with the protagonist as the one culpable, we can yet find comfort in it. The one described by the Lord as 'a man after my own heart' (Acts 13:22) sinned in catastrophic proportions, but God forgave him and had mercy on him. Although we do wrong, we can receive forgiveness and be those characterised as having the heart of the Lord. We can also heed David's example of immediately admitting our wrongs when confronted, without turning to blame or excuses (or better yet, not plotting an intricate cover-up job). Although David suffered earthly consequences for his sin, he remained God's chosen leader for his people.

Today, consider before the Lord any hidden sins that may be lurking in the back of your mind and heart. Ask the Helper, the Holy Spirit, to reveal anything that might be keeping you from communion with God, that you may confess and be released from its power. May we know the joy of being forgiven, cleansed and made new.

## Prayer

*Father God, my heart fills with sadness when I think of the crimes David committed against Bathsheba and Uriah. Though you forgave him, the innocent suffered. This feels wrong—simply wrong. I see it happening in the world, when women and children are raped in war and young boys are turned into soldiers, and it breaks my heart. Have mercy, Lord; have mercy. Show me how to grasp these mysteries, if they are graspable. May you help me to know how I can make a difference in these big situations in the world. Lord, I feel small, and without influence. Help me to know what I can do to be a voice for the voiceless, that I may stand up as their advocate.*

## Thursday

# Communal repentance

'I am too ashamed and disgraced, my God, to lift up my face to you, because our sins are higher than our heads and our guilt has reached to the heavens... Because of our sins, we and our kings and our priests have been subjected to the sword and captivity, to pillage and humiliation at the hand of foreign kings, as it is today...

'But now, our God, what can we say after this? For we have forsaken the commands you gave through your servants the prophets when you said: "The land you are entering to possess is a land polluted by the corruption of its peoples. By their detestable practices they have filled it with their impurity from one end to the other. Therefore, do not give your daughters in marriage to their sons or take their daughters for your sons. Do not seek a treaty of friendship with them at any time, that you may be strong and eat the good things of the land and leave it to your children as an everlasting inheritance."

'What has happened to us is a result of our evil deeds and our great guilt, and yet, our God, you have punished us less than our sins have deserved... Lord, the God of Israel, you are righteous! We are left this day as a remnant. Here we are before you in our guilt, though because of it not one of us can stand in your presence.'

EZRA 9:6–7, 10–13, 15 (abridged)

A church I knew had experienced a period of strife and conflict, and although many people had left and those remaining felt bruised, one Sunday they came together for a service of thanksgiving, repentance and renewal. It was a public way to gather and ask for God's forgiveness for the sinful words and deeds that had passed between people. During the service they prayed together, saying, 'We meet, as generations have met before us, to seek forgiveness for the sin by which we individually and collectively have denied God's claim upon us.' The service was a powerful expression of release, after which the rebuilding commenced.

This act of worship parallels the one we read about in the book of Ezra. God's people had been exiled from the promised land by the king of Babylon; for 70 years they had lived away from the land God gave to them especially as his people. But as prophesied in Jeremiah 25, they returned to Jerusalem in 537BC, and under Ezra and Nehemiah they began to rebuild the walls and make the city habitable again. They came home.

A key part of their return includes a call for national repentance from both Ezra and Nehemiah (these two books in the Bible were originally one) for what the Lord deemed to be the sin of intermarrying with foreign nations; these unions had led to idolatry and an increased emphasis on trading and materialism. Their acts of confession and repentance prove to be a turning point for God's people, for the sin of intermarriage leading to idolatry is thereafter removed from them, no longer proving a hindrance to their commitment to the Lord.

At the beginning of this week we looked at the practice of intermarriage that happened at the time of the prophet Samuel, long before the people of Israel went into exile, and it's worth pointing out here that the Lord forbade it then as a way of keeping his people devoted to him. He understood their weakness and propensity to worship other gods, and if foreign women married into the family without converting to faith in the true and living God, he knew they would soon fall astray. The Lord put rules in place to save them from the heartache of having families that didn't worship him together. However, we also see other instances in scripture where marriage with a foreigner proved successful, such as Boaz the Israelite with Ruth the Moabite.[16]

Ezra's act of public confession on behalf of the community leads the way for God's people to lay firm foundations as they rebuild the city walls. They are clearing out not only the physical rubble but the spiritual as well, as they pave the way for a construction of strong buildings that will withstand future storms. When the people see Ezra outside the temple, weeping and lamenting, their consciences are pricked and they join in the confession.

Thinking back to the church service for repentance and renewal that I described earlier, we don't know how the Lord will answer such prayers, and what might be loosed in heaven as he responds. But we know that he hears our prayer, and that he delights in our turning from deception and sin to a life of holiness and righteousness.

## Prayer

*Powerful and living Lord, I know that the sins committed against you are many, and I have contributed to the wrongdoing through what I have done and what I have failed to do. Forgive me for my sloth when I can't be bothered to act against injustice. Spur me on to love and good deeds, that I might share your grace and truth widely. I also confess the sins committed on a national level, about which you know but I may not. May you release us from our sins, that we may serve you in peace and freedom.*

# Friday

# Set free

Blessed is the one
  whose transgressions are forgiven,
  whose sins are covered.
Blessed is the one
  whose sin the Lord does not count against them
  and in whose spirit is no deceit.
When I kept silent,
  my bones wasted away
  through my groaning all day long.
For day and night
  your hand was heavy on me;
my strength was sapped
  as in the heat of summer.
Then I acknowledged my sin to you
  and did not cover up my iniquity.
I said, 'I will confess
  my transgressions to the Lord.'
And you forgave
  the guilt of my sin.
Therefore let all the faithful pray to you
  while you may be found;
surely the rising of the mighty waters
  will not reach them.
You are my hiding-place;
  you will protect me from trouble
  and surround me with songs of deliverance.

PSALM 32:1–7

The fresh, clean feeling of being forgiven is like no other. Although our emotions may feel raw, when we receive the gift of forgiveness we can have the sense of being scooped up and held, cherished and adored as we are released from our sin. The infraction flies away like a cawing bird who is quietened, never again to hover over us with its burden of guilt and shame. At least, this is the hope and the ideal, but in a fallen world we may not feel that the Lord has forgiven us after we've confessed, fearing that we'll always be defined by our crimes. If we've wronged a friend or family member, they may not want to release us. But the Lord longs that we would enjoy this sense of being washed clean, for through the death of Jesus on the cross we are set free and made new.

The book of Psalms includes seven 'penitential psalms' (Psalms 6, 32, 38, 51, 102, 130 and 143) that express the desire of the author (King David for the majority of them) to confess and receive forgiveness. Psalm 32, however, is the sole one of the seven that shares the feelings he experiences after he's been forgiven, not when waiting to be forgiven. David tells how he sinned, and then how his slate has been wiped clean.

In the first two verses we see three definitions of forgiveness that we can cling to as coming from the heart of the Lord for his people. The first is the literal meaning of the Hebrew word for 'forgiven' (v. 1), which means 'taken away', 'removed'. David knows that his sins are now as far from him as the east is from the west (see Psalm 103:12). He's not defined by them: he's not known in the Bible as a murderer, but as a man after God's own heart. For us who call on the name of the Lord, Jesus removed the power of our sins when he died in our place. He took our place so that our sins would no longer bind us.

The second meaning of forgiveness, again in verse 1, entails our sins being 'covered'. As dirt can put out a fire, extinguishing the flames that threaten to burn and destroy, so can the Lord cover our sins. As Jesus was buried in the tomb, so are our transgressions deposited far from us.

The third meaning is that our sins are uncounted (v. 2). The Lord doesn't keep a grand tally of our wrongdoings, wondering if we'll change. Rather, when he forgives us he really does wipe our slate clean.

Jesus as our Advocate before the Father not only argues our case but has taken on our guilty verdict.[17]

Have you received the Lord's forgiveness this day?

## Prayer

*Lord God, blessed and joyful am I whose transgressions are forgiven, whose sins are covered. You don't count my sins against me, and you release me from my self-deception. When I acknowledge my sin to you, you take away my guilt and shame. Therefore let me pray to you where you may be found, for you are my hiding-place; you protect me from trouble and surround me with songs of deliverance. You teach me in the way I should go; you counsel me and keep your loving eye always on me. Lord, I want not to be like a mule with no understanding, who has to be controlled with a bit in its mouth, for I want to learn from you. Your unfailing love surrounds me, and I trust in you. I rejoice and am glad; I sing with joy and purity of heart.*

# Saturday

# The covering of love

Whoever would foster love covers over an offence,
  but whoever repeats the matter separates close friends.
PROVERBS 17:9

Hatred stirs up conflict,
  but love covers over all wrongs.
PROVERBS 10:12

A perverse person stirs up conflict,
  and a gossip separates close friends.
PROVERBS 16:28

A person's wisdom yields patience;
  it is to one's glory to overlook an offence.
PROVERBS 19:11

I felt helpless when my friend was the subject of perilous gossip. What was being whispered from person to person was based on speculation, not fact. But as she had taken me into her confidence, I couldn't say anything to put the facts straight when the subject came up. When someone started to muse about what they thought had happened, I would pray under my breath and try to shift the conversation to other topics. During that rough time, my friend was an inspiration and example to me. Although I was stung by the rumours on her behalf, she said she had forgiven the one who was spreading the gossip. She seemed to have received a special deposit of grace from which to forgive and release the one speaking against her.

My friend wasn't letting the gossip bring her down; she covered over the offence and moved on. She could have easily started her own rumours in revenge, stirring up conflict, but she kept her head down and in time the matter blew over. Even so, I knew that although she had been able to forgive, the gossip had wounded her tender heart. I ached for her, thinking just how destructive loose words are, and how they can separate friends and neighbours. I prayed that the Lord would continue to bring healing as he applied his balm to her hurts.

By standing in truth and keeping quiet, my friend exemplified the wisdom in the proverbs we look at today. They are among the sayings written by King Solomon, David's son, who was known for his wisdom. The main author of this book of the Bible, he wrote and collected 3000 proverbs (see 1 Kings 4:32) as a way of passing along his wisdom and teaching the young. The book is filled with pithy words on topics about how to live—and on how fools go about their business.

We see in these sayings not only instruction for life, but the wisdom of forgiveness—how a wise person takes their time before replying and covers over the offence (more of the language of 'covering', as we saw yesterday with Psalm 32). Peter echoes Proverbs 10:12 in his first letter when he emphasises the value of love in forgiveness: 'Above all, love each other deeply, because love covers over a multitude of sins' (1 Peter 4:8).

How can we keep these proverbs in mind today? We could ask the Holy Spirit to make us aware when we should hold back from uttering a comment that is on the tip of our tongue. When we submit to his leading, he can keep us from messing up and saying something that might incite pain. Or we could take some positive action to combat the gossip that so easily moves from one person to another, instead finding ways to spread wholesome stories about people. Just think of all of the good that could come from a healthy sharing of anecdotes that build others up.

May we be those who promote whatever is true, noble, right, pure, lovely, admirable, excellent and praiseworthy (Philippians 4:8).

## Prayer

*Lord Jesus Christ, you were the subject of malicious talk—and worse. Help me to forgive those who slander me, that I will not be enslaved to bitterness, but will be free to live and love and stand in my identity as your beloved and forgiven child. I long for a world where gossip doesn't reign and people aren't wounded by words that are used as weapons. I ache at the hurt and betrayal I witness and sometimes experience. May I be one who doesn't let any unwholesome talk come out of my mouth, but only what is helpful for building up others according to their needs and your glory.*

# Spiritual exercises and questions for individual reflection and group discussion

## Growth following scars

You will need a small pot; compost; pea seeds; paper.

The Israelites under King Saul didn't worship the Lord wholeheartedly, and their sins resulted in spiritual scars. We too receive scars when we turn from the Lord or when people wound us.

Take some time in prayer, considering any scars or wounds that you would like to offer to God. Write a prayer on a piece of paper about any hurt that remains, confessing if necessary how you could have acted differently. Fold up the paper and put it at the bottom of the pot, covering it with compost. Plant the pea seeds and welcome the growth and new life that God can bring, even out of a scarring experience.

If you and a small group do this exercise towards the beginning of Lent, encourage the members to bring their plants back to the group after a few weeks so that all can witness the shoots and leaves. People can also share about the growth in their lives.[18]

## Clean slate

You will need a blackboard and chalk or a whiteboard and pens; a camera.

As you consider how David sinned, and yet how the Lord called him 'a man after his own heart', read Psalm 51. Consider the words he uses, including sin, evil, transgressions, verdict, judge; blot, restore, sustain, deliver, teach, wash away, cleanse; and mercy, unfailing love, compassion, joy, gladness, righteousness, contrite.

Thinking of these words, write on your board any of the negative words that resonate from the psalm or any sins you want to be free of. Ask God to take them away from you, wiping your slate clean, as you wipe them away with a cloth. Wait before the Lord, asking the Holy Spirit to show you any words, songs or pictures he has for you, and write them on the board (perhaps these will be some of the life-giving words from Psalm 51). Take a photo as a memory of your clean slate that the Lord wants to fill with good and beautiful things.[19]

## Praying for your enemies

Perhaps you've been the subject of gossip, as I described on Saturday with my friend's situation. If not, perhaps you have been sinned against in other ways. Ask God to help you pray for your enemies or for those who have mistreated you. Ask the Lord to bless them, that they would come to know him or deepen their relationship with him; that they would have strong relationships with the people close to them; that they would flourish in their place of work or study or community; that you would be free of bitterness against them, and that you would be able to wish them well.

## Questions for reflection and discussion

- Why do you think the Israelites so longed for a king? In Saul we see some negative outcomes of having one, but can you think of positive outcomes as well?
- Abigail acted on behalf of Nabal and prevented bloodshed—as well as keeping David's reputation intact. What struck you in this story?
- 'You are the man,' said Nathan, and David repented immediately and fully. Though he bore the consequences of his lies and murder,

he remained committed to God. Were you surprised that the Lord spoke through Nathan in this fashion? How do you think David felt when he heard that he had been found out?

- The Israelites repented of their half-heartedness, as we saw in the passage we read from the book of Ezra. What do you think caused them to rend their garments and return to the Lord? Have you ever witnessed or experienced a similar corporate wave of repentance? How can we pray for a move of the Spirit in this way?

- You may use the Psalms to help you praise the Lord, but have you ever employed any of the seven penitential psalms (Psalms 6, 32, 38, 51, 102, 130 and 143) to aid your prayers of confession?

# Week 3

# The Prophets:
# Calling God's People to Return

In Week 3 we encounter six prophets—men the Lord uses to call his people back to him. They seek Israel's repentance, that God's people will turn from their false gods and idols to serve the true and living God with their whole heart. We see Isaiah, who confronts King Hezekiah with his sins; Jeremiah, who rebukes God's people through the image of clay jars; Daniel, who repents on behalf of a nation; Hosea, who obeys God and aligns himself with a fallen woman for her redemption; Jonah, who obeys God yet doesn't voice his repentance; and Micah, who laments for God's people and seeks their repentance.

The prophets speak words of judgement and yet hope, foreshadowing the confession we can make and the forgiveness we receive at the cross, where we are freed from, not judged for, our sins. Through Jesus' sacrifice, we find our slates washed clean and we can embrace the gift of freedom and new life.

This week, note some of the images and symbols that the prophets employ, such as sins being made white as snow, sins being put behind God's back, the jars of clay, and Jonah's withered plant. Consider how these images enhance your understanding of God's redeeming work.

## Sunday

# Made white as snow

Stop bringing meaningless offerings!
　　Your incense is detestable to me.
New Moons, Sabbaths and convocations—
　　I cannot bear your worthless assemblies.
Your New Moon feasts and your appointed festivals
　　I hate with all my being.
They have become a burden to me;
　　I am weary of bearing them.
When you spread out your hands in prayer,
　　I hide my eyes from you;
even when you offer many prayers,
　　I am not listening.
Your hands are full of blood!
　　Wash and make yourselves clean.
Take your evil deeds out of my sight;
　　stop doing wrong.
Learn to do right; seek justice.
　　Defend the oppressed.
Take up the cause of the fatherless;
　　plead the case of the widow.
'Come now, let us settle the matter,'
　　says the Lord.
'Though your sins are like scarlet,
　　they shall be as white as snow;
though they are red as crimson,
　　they shall be like wool.
If you are willing and obedient,
　　you will eat the good things of the land.
ISAIAH 1:13–19

'Who is the more religious of the two of you, you or your husband?' the radio interviewer asked.

I was taken aback, but answered, 'I think we both have a strong and committed faith, and that's one of the reasons I was so drawn to him at the start.'

As I reflected later, I realised that even on a BBC Sunday morning show, I was seen as 'religious', which is not a word I would normally use to describe myself. A committed Christian, yes; one who loves the Lord and seeks to follow him. But religious? That seems to make me either too holy to handle or as if I mindlessly follow empty rituals.

Yet this is how so much of society sees Christians: we're religious, especially if we take part in what they would call 'organised religion' (I was on the show talking about being a vicar's wife, so that doubly categorised me). They may believe we have signed up to a life of rules and regulations. Unfortunately, with these characterisations they miss out on understanding the intimacy we Christians can feel with God because of our relationship with him.

This relationship is what the Lord urges his people to return to in our reading from the prophet Isaiah. The Lord speaks through the prophet, telling the Israelites that he takes no pleasure in their offerings or incense, their assemblies and festivals. Rather he is burdened by them, for the Israelites' hearts are not pure. Instead of pursuing a relationship with God in which they look inside and confess any wrongdoing that may be keeping them from wholehearted devotion to the Lord, they rely on the outward action of following the rules. Keeping rules can be easier than confessing one's secret sins.

But the Lord sees the state of their hearts and speaks his word. He calls them to right living, which includes seeking justice and defending the weak. He wants them to argue their case before him so that he may turn their scarlet sins as white as snow. When they repent, he will restore them to a right relationship with him; they will 'eat the best from the land', which hints of the feasting that the Lord welcomes them to enjoy.

How about us? We know that Jesus himself was the final sacrifice on the cross, so we aren't required to offer bulls or rams to the Lord. But we might think that we have to sacrifice offerings to the Lord in other ways in order to be close to him. Or we might hide behind rituals or regulations, imagining that this is safer than baring our heart, fears and emotions to the Lord. Or we might not believe that we're truly forgiven, thinking that we'll always be marked with scarlet sins.

Yet Jesus' work on the cross frees us. His cross is living, for through it we can stand tall in our identity as God's beloved children, washed free and made as white as snow. And maybe, as we share the love we receive from God, people in society will learn that we are Christians—not by our rituals, but by our love.

## Prayer

*Father God, sometimes I hide behind rules, thinking that if I keep them, you will accept me. But you have already beckoned me to yourself, running towards me when I return home. Help me to deepen my relationship with you, that my good works will flow from a grateful heart. Wash me clean, Lord, that I may no longer cling to any scarlet sins, but may know freedom and release. I ask for a fresh infilling of your Spirit, that I would be marked by your love and able to extend it to those I meet.*

## Monday

# Putting our sins behind his back

In those days Hezekiah became ill and was at the point of death. The prophet Isaiah son of Amoz went to him and said, 'This is what the Lord says: put your house in order, because you are going to die; you will not recover.'

Hezekiah turned his face to the wall and prayed to the Lord, 'Remember, Lord, how I have walked before you faithfully and with wholehearted devotion and have done what is good in your eyes.' And Hezekiah wept bitterly.

Then the word of the Lord came to Isaiah: 'Go and tell Hezekiah, "This is what the Lord, the God of your father David, says: I have heard your prayer and seen your tears; I will add fifteen years to your life. And I will deliver you and this city from the hand of the king of Assyria. I will defend this city..."'

A writing of Hezekiah king of Judah after his illness and recovery:

... But what can I say?
    He has spoken to me, and he himself has done this.
I will walk humbly all my years
    because of this anguish of my soul.
Lord, by such things people live;
    and my spirit finds life in them too.
You restored me to health
    and let me live.
Surely it was for my benefit
    that I suffered such anguish.
In your love you kept me
    from the pit of destruction;
you have put all my sins
    behind your back.

ISAIAH 38:1–6, 9, 15–17

As I read Hezekiah's plea to the Lord, some lyrics of a gospel blues song keep running through my mind: 'I know God; he don't never change; God: he always will be God.'[20] It's true that the Lord won't change; from everlasting to everlasting, his goodness remains (Malachi 3:6).

And yet, and yet... How amazing it is that although the goodness and loving-kindness of the Lord stays the same, yet because of his great mercy the God of the universe can and does change his mind, as we see with Hezekiah. Though the Lord had decreed that the king of Judah would die, Hezekiah cries out with eloquence and passion, stating that he has followed God wholeheartedly. The Lord relents, adding 15 years to his life.

Hezekiah responds with a song of love and lament. Though life is fleeting, the Lord saves him. The Lord answers his request, and he will therefore live humbly and with thanks. He responds with this evocative line: 'In your love you kept me from the pit of destruction; you have put all my sins behind your back' (v. 17).

What a wonderful image! We might try to escape our sins by pushing them under a carpet or sweeping them into the corner of a room, but they can tumble out and control us. We might try turning our back on our sins, shielding our eyes from their gruesomeness. But only through Jesus bearing our sins on *his* back on the cross will we be made free, for this is how the Father puts our sins behind his back. Then we will no longer be known by the false names we take on or are given, such as Liar, Useless, Cheat, Gossip or Guilty One. Instead we are washed free, able to live out of our identity as Beloved, Warrior, Delighted in, Chosen.

Today, consider the image of your sins being put behind God's back. How does that feel?

## Prayer

*Lord Jesus, as I contemplate your sacrifice, I am humbled. I'm sorry that my sins and wrongdoing sent you to the cross, but I am grateful that through your death they no longer bind or control me. I am free, and I am forgiven. I can stand tall, knowing that I'm no longer dirty, but cleansed and washed. My sins are behind the Father's back. Help me to forgive as I have been forgiven; to extend mercy and grace when I might be tempted to exact revenge. I don't want to become bitter or ensnared by my sins, but I want to live in the light of your love, that I may share this love with others. May it be so this day.*

# Tuesday

# Jars of clay

This is what the Lord says: 'Go and buy a clay jar from a potter. Take along some of the elders of the people and of the priests and go out to the Valley of Ben Hinnom, near the entrance of the Potsherd Gate. There proclaim the words I tell you, and say, "Hear the word of the Lord, you kings of Judah and people of Jerusalem. This is what the Lord Almighty, the God of Israel, says: listen! I am going to bring a disaster on this place that will make the ears of everyone who hears of it tingle. For they have forsaken me and made this a place of foreign gods; they have burned incense in it to gods that neither they nor their ancestors nor the kings of Judah ever knew, and they have filled this place with the blood of the innocent. They have built the high places of Baal to burn their children in the fire as offerings to Baal—something I did not command or mention, nor did it enter my mind. So beware, the days are coming, declares the Lord, when people will no longer call this place Topheth or the Valley of Ben Hinnom, but the Valley of Slaughter...

'Then break the jar while those who go with you are watching, and say to them, "This is what the Lord Almighty says: I will smash this nation and this city just as this potter's jar is smashed and cannot be repaired."'

JEREMIAH 19:1–6, 10–11

I once took a pottery class and struggled to shape a pot that wasn't an ugly lump of hardened clay, good only for the incinerator. But during the last fortnight of the class, I had a breakthrough on the wheel and finally could shape a passable vessel. With delight I worked long into the night, enjoying the feeling of moulding the wet clay into vases, bowls and other shapes. Although they would be loved only by their creator, they brought me joy and fulfilment.

Even though Israel is the Lord's beloved clay jar, time and time again she fails her God. She pursues other loves, other idols. And although the Lord forgives, he also declares his judgement, as we see in this passage from the prophet Jeremiah. The Lord tells him to enact a parable, so that the people would understand the harm caused by their actions. 'Go and get an earthenware vessel, a clay jar,' says the Lord, 'and shatter it in front of the leaders of the people, that they might understand the message of judgement.'

These instructions contain meaning that may remain hidden to us. For instance, the place where Jeremiah and the elders go to smash the pot is important, for the Valley of Ben Hinnom was not only close to the potter's house but had also become associated with child sacrifice. The Lord makes it clear that this detestable practice is unacceptable for his people. The smashing of the clay jar is filled with significance as well, for when someone wronged another, the abused party would take a clay jar and smash it next to the perpetrator, implying that they wished the same fate on the one who had caused them harm. Jeremiah thus delivers God's verdict on his people: because of their sins, they will be smashed to pieces.[21]

Taken alone, this passage may dishearten us. Where, we might wonder, is God's mercy and love? How about the people's repentance, which could usher them into new life? We who live in the shadow of the cross know that God works redemption for our good, but because of this sure knowledge we sometimes rush too quickly to the 'forgiven' part of the equation. Lent is a good time to consider our wrongs—not in a self-flagellating sort of way, but so that we can turn from them and receive God's forgiveness.

Where has the clay of our lives become dry and hardened? Have we, through our habits and actions, turned into a misshapen vessel? Consider the Potter, who will make our clay malleable and moist, if we only ask him to come and have his way in our lives. He can turn us into vessels that bring glory to him as we hold his living water, his unsurpassable glory, even in these jars of clay (see 2 Corinthians 4:7).

He who makes designs like no other artist will take delight in forming us into his beautiful and useful creation.

## Prayer

*Lord God, search my heart for any hidden or lurking sins that keep me from loving you. May you reveal them gently, showing me where I've gone wrong and what I can do to turn from them. May you help me to present them to your Son on the cross, that I might be free of their power over me. Help me if this step feels too large, so that I can find a starting point. I ask you to forgive me and help me to receive your gifts of love, affirmation, healing and grace to fill those places where my sin's tentacles reach so deeply. May I know your freedom; may I know your peace. May I share this holy, healing love with those I've wronged, where bitterness has come between me and another.*

# Wednesday

# 'Lord, forgive!'

I prayed to the Lord my God and confessed:

'Lord, the great and awesome God, who keeps his covenant of love with those who love him and keep his commandments, we have sinned and done wrong. We have been wicked and have rebelled; we have turned away from your commands and laws. We have not listened to your servants the prophets, who spoke in your name to our kings, our princes and our ancestors, and to all the people of the land.

'Lord, you are righteous, but this day we are covered with shame... We and our kings, our princes and our ancestors are covered with shame, Lord, because we have sinned against you. The Lord our God is merciful and forgiving, even though we have rebelled against him; we have not obeyed the Lord our God or kept the laws he gave us through his servants the prophets. All Israel has transgressed your law and turned away, refusing to obey you...

'Now, our God, hear the prayers and petitions of your servant. For your sake, Lord, look with favour on your desolate sanctuary. Give ear, our God, and hear; open your eyes and see the desolation of the city that bears your Name. We do not make requests of you because we are righteous, but because of your great mercy. Lord, listen! Lord, forgive! Lord, hear and act! For your sake, my God, do not delay, because your city and your people bear your Name.'

DANIEL 9:4–11, 17–19 (abridged)

Fifty years after Uganda gained independence from British rule, the nation's president repented publicly of his sins and the sins of the nation, asking God to forgive them. At a prayer gathering, he prayed: 'I stand here today to close the evil past, and especially in the last 50 years of our national leadership history... We confess sins of idolatry and witchcraft which are rampant in our land. We confess sins of shedding innocent blood, sins of political hypocrisy, dishonesty, intrigue and betrayal...'[22]

Not everyone thought the Ugandan president should be repenting on behalf of the nation, but he had a strong biblical example in the book of Daniel. While in exile, Daniel reads the scriptures and realises that God's people will be in exile for 70 years. In sackcloth and ashes he immediately turns to the Lord in repentance on behalf of the people, crying out to God for mercy and release. His prayers are heartfelt and deep, for he longs that God's people will be forgiven and brought back to the land that God promised them.

Note (and do read the full text of verses 1–19 if you can) that Daniel doesn't excuse their actions. He doesn't blame others or reason away their sins, but gives a passionate and heartfelt confession on behalf of God's people. Although he himself isn't personally implicated, he doesn't shirk the sense of responsibility for shouldering their sins.

Daniel knows that any forgiveness the Lord gives will be because of his great mercy, and not because the people deserve forgiveness (v. 18). But he comes before the Lord boldly, asking for God's pardon for the people because they bear his name. As we see in the verses following the passage printed above, the Lord answers quickly in sending the angel Gabriel, even before Daniel has finished his prayers and petitions, to say that he will bring the 70 years of captivity to an end.

I wonder how the lives of Ugandans were different after the president's act of repentance. I wonder too how the lives of our nations might be different if we came before the Lord on our knees, confessing the ways in which our laws and customs transgress the Lord's commands. We know that the Lord answers prayers, and we see with Daniel how God moved swiftly to bring an end to their exile. How much may be released through prayer is a mystery that we'll never fully understand, but we know that our heavenly Father is good and loving and will answer our pleas and petitions according to his great mercy.

## Prayer

*Father God, loving Son, comforting Spirit, I come before you in sadness for the atrocities I see committed around the world, and for the things in my locality that grieve you. Hear me when I pray, for I call on your name. Have mercy, in keeping with your righteous acts. May I bring you not shame or scorn, but glory. Hear my petitions and prayers, not because I am righteous but because you are merciful and loving. O Lord, listen! O Lord, forgive! O Lord, hear and act! For your name's sake; do not delay. I ask in your holy name, and for your sake.*

## Thursday

# Returning home

Return, Israel, to the Lord your God.
　　Your sins have been your downfall!
Take words with you
　　and return to the Lord.
Say to him:
　　'Forgive all our sins
and receive us graciously,
　　that we may offer the fruit of our lips.
Assyria cannot save us;
　　we will not mount war-horses.
We will never again say "Our gods"
　　to what our own hands have made,
　　for in you the fatherless find compassion.'

'I will heal their waywardness
　　and love them freely,
　　for my anger has turned away from them.
I will be like the dew to Israel;
　　he will blossom like a lily.
Like a cedar of Lebanon
　　he will send down his roots;
　　his young shoots will grow.
His splendour will be like an olive tree,
　　his fragrance like a cedar of Lebanon.
People will dwell again in his shade;
　　they will flourish like the corn,
they will blossom like the vine—
　　Israel's fame will be like the wine of Lebanon.
Ephraim, what more have I to do with idols?
　　I will answer him and care for him.

I am like a flourishing juniper;
>    your fruitfulness comes from me.'
HOSEA 14:1–8

In an age when people share intimate secrets online, we can find blogs written under a pseudonym by people who have had affairs, have repented and are now working to save their marriages. One is by a man called Sean, who tells how his wife accepted him back after he had been cheating on her for a year. As he says in a post, although in a Hollywood movie we'd witness a tearful reunion followed by the closing credits, in real life many more tough scenes follow a reconciliation as the couple work to re-establish intimacy and trust.[23] The damage of dalliances runs deep.

When we see the pain caused by adultery, we may be puzzled by the book of Hosea, for the Lord called this prophet to marry a promiscuous woman. We may wonder why God would ask him to do so, for obeying this call would entail welcoming heartache and rejection into his life. But as we see in the earlier chapters of the book, Hosea doesn't put forth queries or concerns but obeys, marrying Gomer. She bears him children, but she also strays from the marriage covenant.

The book reveals on a human level some of the anguish that the Lord feels for his people, who continue to turn from him in their pursuit of other loves. It embodies a symbol of love between God and his people, which we also see in the Song of Songs—the image of bride and bridegroom, beloved and lover. Thus the Lord puts himself under the power of the bride, feeling rejection and pain when she spurns him. Though he is the all-powerful God, the Creator of the universe, yet he seeks the love of his people. As I reflect on this mystery, I echo the words of King David: 'Such knowledge is too wonderful for me, too lofty for me to attain' (Psalm 139:6).

In chapter 14, the final chapter of the book of Hosea, we hear the Lord deliver words of absolution, forgiveness and healing if the people will repent. If they will turn from idols, from worshipping the things they've created, the Lord will welcome them back and make them fruitful. When we read about idols, do we consign that idea to past times and past peoples who created objects out of gold? Or do we recognise where we have given our heart over to modern-day idols, such as influence, success, power, money, affirmation or something else? Can we say with the Israelites, 'Never again' (v. 3) as we keep our love-relationship with God pure?

God's promises of gracious forgiveness can be as a balm to our soul. Perhaps take a few moments to ponder the following phrases, which are all from this text, and let them sink into your soul. The Lord will heal our waywardness and love us freely. He turns away his anger. We will blossom as a lily or a vine. Like a strong tree we will send down our roots, with shoots of growth and splendour as we flourish and are fruitful.

Though we sin and bring pain to the Lord, he delights to bestow forgiveness to us, that our relationship with him would be restored. May it be so this day.

## Prayer

*Lord God, you are holy and wonderful, and the fact that you love me without end brings me comfort and security. When I've turned away from you, please woo me and bring me back home. I'm sorry for the times when I've sought meaning and fulfilment elsewhere. Forgive me and restore me, that I might know contentment with you. You love me freely; you receive me graciously. May your love be the solid foundation of meaning and hope in my life so that, knowing who I am as your beloved, I may share this love with others.*

# Friday

# The reluctant prophet

Then the word of the Lord came to Jonah a second time: 'Go to the great city of Nineveh and proclaim to it the message I give you.'

Jonah obeyed the word of the Lord and went to Nineveh... Jonah began by going a day's journey into the city, proclaiming, 'Forty more days and Nineveh will be overthrown.' The Ninevites believed God. A fast was proclaimed, and all of them, from the greatest to the least, put on sackcloth.

When Jonah's warning reached the king of Nineveh, he rose from his throne, took off his royal robes, covered himself with sackcloth and sat down in the dust. This is the proclamation he issued in Nineveh:

'By the decree of the king and his nobles: Do not let people or animals, herds or flocks, taste anything; do not let them eat or drink. But let people and animals be covered with sackcloth. Let everyone call urgently on God. Let them give up their evil ways and their violence. Who knows? God may yet relent and with compassion turn from his fierce anger so that we will not perish.'

When God saw what they did and how they turned from their evil ways, he relented and did not bring on them the destruction he had threatened.

JONAH 3:1–10 (abridged)

When I first moved to England, I felt I was obeying the call of God. I had sensed his clear guidance to marry my English husband and become, like Abraham, a 'stranger in a foreign country' (Hebrews 11:9). The thought of making a home on the other side of the Atlantic had a tinge of glamour and excitement when it was only a thought. After the joy of the wedding and the intense activity of executing an international move, however, when the thought became a reality, I wondered what I had signed up for. Yes, I was married to my Englishman, but when I experienced a profound sense of culture shock, I began to wonder if I would ever feel at home. I had to train myself not to think about 'doing a runner' like Jonah.[24]

He is sometimes called a 'reluctant prophet', for instead of obeying the Lord's command to preach a message of repentance to the Ninevites, Jonah boards a ship going in the opposite direction. After facing death by being thrown overboard from the boat and, famously, being swallowed up by a big fish,[25] he hears again the command of the Lord to proclaim the message to them. He obeys this time, speaking of impending doom. Amazingly—even miraculously—the Ninevites repent, with everyone fasting, turning from their evil ways and asking God to be merciful. The Lord relents and saves them from death.

But does Jonah delight in God's saving grace? As we see in chapter 5, no. He's angry, huffing and puffing in protest. And note that although he obeys God the second time, we never hear him express emotions of sorrow or regret. Nor do we see him confess his bad attitude after God sends him an object lesson with the plant that withers. It seems that he's still a reluctant vessel for God's message.

I find it encouraging to think that the Lord in his mercy can use us for his purposes when we're obedient but perhaps not totally happy about following his prompts and requests. As I think back to my early days in Cambridge, for example, I remember crying many tears of frustration. But through the weeks, months and years, the Lord has shaped my emotions, helping me to see how he has been with me during this sojourn into a foreign country that has become my home.

And the people of Nineveh? They repented and lived—a change of heart that brought about life.

## Prayer

*Father God, I can relate to Jonah. Sometimes I want to sulk in the corner, wondering why you restore people who don't seem to deserve your grace and love. Or I obey you, but inwardly I'm not happy about it. When I'm wallowing in unhealthy emotions, please take me outside myself, helping me to understand just a hint of your divine perspective, for you are God and I am not, and I don't know all that you know. Change my heart, Lord, that I may be pliable and malleable, willing to be moulded and used for your glory. Help me to rejoice when you extend your saving hand—even if I don't like those whom you've saved.*

## Saturday

# The Forgiveness Project

Who is a God like you,
  who pardons sin and forgives the transgression
  of the remnant of his inheritance?
You do not stay angry for ever
  but delight to show mercy.
You will again have compassion on us;
  you will tread our sins underfoot
  and hurl all our iniquities into the depths of the sea.
You will be faithful to Jacob,
  and show love to Abraham,
as you pledged on oath to our ancestors
  in days long ago.
MICAH 7:18–20

Christians advocate forgiveness because we follow a forgiving God. But some people believe that 'Christians have no monopoly on forgiveness', a statement that characterises Marina Cantacuzino's view.[26] She's the founder of the 'Forgiveness Project', a secular organisation that seeks to foster the sharing of stories about forgiveness. The book of the same name is filled with heartrending stories from around the world of forgiveness extended for murder, rape, kidnapping, alcoholism and many other crimes and issues.

For instance, Wilma Derksen tells of the disappearance of her 13-year-old daughter, who was raped and murdered. On the night they received the horrific news, she and her husband made a decision to forgive the perpetrators after they heard the story of one of their visitors. He too was a father of a murdered child, but not only had he lost his daughter, he'd lost his health, relationships, concentration and even the memory of his daughter, for he could now only think of her brutal killing and not of who she had been. The aftermath of the murder had taken his life.

In the light of what they witnessed in his life, Wilma and her husband vowed to forgive, saying 'no' to anger and obsession. They determined 'to resist anything that would keep us in a state of emotional bondage'.[27] But little did she know, Wilma says, 'that the word "forgiveness" would haunt me for the next 30 years—prod me, guide me, heal me, label me, enlighten me, imprison me, free me and, in the end, define me'. She sees forgiveness as 'a fresh, ongoing, ever-present position of mind… It's a promise of what we want to do, a goal'.[28]

The stories in the book are powerful because they tell of lives transformed as those who forgive are freed from the prison of bitterness and regret. They illustrate the wisdom of God's ways—that we are set free when we model his actions and extend forgiveness. And I agree that we Christians don't have to think that we have a monopoly on forgiveness, as Cantacuzino attests. Though we believe that the Lord is the source of forgiveness, it's a practice that he makes available to all people, whether or not they follow him.[29]

We see how he is a forgiving God in the final verses of Micah's prophecy. After Micah's prayer of lament for God's people, who appear not to repent, he turns to prayers of petition and finally to exclamations of praise and wonder. Is there any other God, he says, than one like the Lord who pardons sins, doesn't stay angry, and delights to show mercy? Micah vividly pictures the Lord drowning our wrongdoings in the depths of the sea, never to trouble us again. Why? Because of his faithful love, which he has pledged and shown for centuries.

No, those who follow the true and living God don't hold a monopoly on forgiveness. If we tried to hoard it only for ourselves, we'd be working against the gracious gift that it is. After all, forgiveness begets forgiveness, for as we give and receive, we want others to experience the freedom it bestows.

## Prayer

*Triune Lord, you are the source of all things and the reason I can forgive. Thank you that you spread this gift so liberally in the world, and that it's not exclusive to those who follow you. I pray that more and more people will open the package of forgiveness, not fearing to lift out the gifts within it. May acts of kindness and forgiveness reverberate throughout the land and the world, that we might live in freedom and peace. May this gift be a gentle prod for people to come to know you and your Son Jesus, who showed us the ultimate act of forgiveness.*

# Spiritual exercises and questions for individual reflection and group discussion

## Praying at the wall

You will need paper and pen; a wall of some kind.

The Western Wall in Jerusalem is known by many Christians as the Wailing Wall, but the name is now becoming less common as it can be seen as derogatory. The wall has served as a safe space for people to let out their heartbreak and anguish over the centuries and is a surviving remnant of God's temple. It forms part of the external wall enclosing the Holy of Holies, the place where God's presence dwelled.

Use the exercise of praying at the wall as a conduit of God's mercy, thinking of God's prophets and their words of grace and judgement to his people. Find a wall with cracks in it, or fashion your own wall out of stones. On slips of paper, write any names or situations that you want to give to the Lord and as you place them into the wall, know that the Lord receives the cries of your heart. Wait for any words, pictures or scriptures that the Lord may have for you.

As you reflect on the exercise, consider if and how you incorporate rituals into your life. If you don't like regular acts of prayer according to certain practices, why not? If you do, what are they? How do they help with any grief and suffering you may experience?

# The potter and the clay

You will need modelling clay, tools such as a rolling pin and cutlery.

As we see in Jeremiah's prophecy, God is the potter and we are the clay. Take some modelling clay as a symbol of your malleable heart being held in the potter's hands. As you mould the clay, think of any areas of hard-heartedness or bitterness that you would like to see gone, any places of pain that seem to be festering, or any stubborn traits that you long to be free of.

As you shape and mould, ask God to make your heart similarly pliable. Form the clay into the shape of a heart, not despairing if you do so imperfectly. Know that the Lord is with you and within you, transforming you with his presence.[30]

# Lectio divina

You will need a Bible; paper and pen.

*Lectio divina*, a Latin phrase for the act of sacred reading, is the ancient practice of a slow, contemplative praying of the scriptures, which can cause a merely rational process to move deep into one's heart. This practice can be summed up as the four Rs—reading, reflecting, responding and resting—but it's a circular process, so we might move from one stage back to another, and then jump down to another, as inspired by the Spirit.

Choose a passage of scripture, such as this week's readings from Daniel, Hosea or Micah, and slowly engage with the four steps. First, read the passage while listening with expectancy and holy reverence. Second, meditate on the words, in the same way as an animal chews its cud. Take in the word and turn it over, gently repeating it and letting it interact with your thoughts, hopes, memories and desires. Third, pray, making your response to God as you offer to him thanksgiving, praise, petition, repentance and adoration. Fourth, stop in the presence of the loving Father. Words are not necessary as you rest without striving and practise silence, simply enjoying the presence of God.

Move through these steps with your text, pausing and reflecting and mining the riches of God's word. Afterwards, consider what struck you in a new way. Were you able to rest and receive?

# Questions for reflection and discussion

- What do you think about society's use of the terms 'spiritual' and 'religious'? How do you describe yourself?
- What speaks to you as you read the passage from Jeremiah about the potter and the clay? How does this use of the image contrast to the one we find in Isaiah 64:8?
- Imagine what a national act of repentance would look like in your country. How might things change? How can you play a role in such confession on a larger scale?
- How do you view God's call to Hosea to marry a promiscuous woman? What effect did this marriage have on Gomer, and on Hosea?
- Marina Cantacuzino says Christians don't have a 'monopoly on forgiveness.' Do you agree or disagree? Why?

# Week 4

# Jesus Forgives

We move from the Old Testament stories, which all point to our need for a Saviour, to the New, where we meet this very Saviour, Jesus the Messiah. This is the God-man who came to live as one of us and to die in our place so that he could free us from our selfishness, pride, gossip, anger and other sins.

Our first encounter with Jesus reveals just how unique he is. During his first instance of public ministry, he reads from the prophet Isaiah in the synagogue and announces his coming as the Messiah. His is a message of forgiveness and release.

During the week, we read some stories of Jesus transforming the lives of people he meets, such as the Samaritan woman who longs for living water, the paralysed man lowered through the roof, and the woman who anoints him with oil from an alabaster jar. We also learn from his teaching in the Sermon on the Mount and through his parable of the unforgiving servant.

We see in various ways how Jesus forgives through his great love for those he encounters, a deep love he extends to his followers throughout the generations. He longs that we would find forgiveness through his freeing act on the cross, for there we can find new life.

# Sunday

# The Anointed One

Jesus returned to Galilee in the power of the Spirit, and news about him spread through the whole countryside. He was teaching in their synagogues, and everyone praised him.

He went to Nazareth, where he had been brought up, and on the Sabbath day he went into the synagogue, as was his custom. He stood up to read, and the scroll of the prophet Isaiah was handed to him. Unrolling it, he found the place where it is written:

'The Spirit of the Lord is on me,
    because he has anointed me
    to proclaim good news to the poor.
He has sent me to proclaim freedom for the prisoners
    and recovery of sight for the blind,
to set the oppressed free,
    to proclaim the year of the Lord's favour.'

Then he rolled up the scroll, gave it back to the attendant and sat down. The eyes of everyone in the synagogue were fastened on him. He began by saying to them, 'Today this scripture is fulfilled in your hearing.'
LUKE 4:14–21

When I was a student in the States, I spent some time on a course called 'Law in London'. I attended a Christian university but joined a range of students from other Minnesota universities on the course in the capital city. When one of them asked me where I attended, I told him and he responded with, 'Oh, the university for religious freaks.' I felt stunned by his assessment and tried to protest, but wasn't sure how to handle it. I understood in a flash how Jesus can divide.

Jesus, having been tested in the wilderness and now full of the power of the Spirit, returns to his humble home town to commence his public ministry. At the synagogue, on the sabbath, he takes part in the service, reading from the prophet at the customary point. We can see God's hand in this key moment, for the appointed text that day is from Isaiah (61:1–2), in which Jesus announces that salvation has come to God's people. In a statement that penetrates the hearts of the listeners, he proclaims, 'Today this scripture is fulfilled in your hearing.'

Jesus calls himself the Messiah, the long-awaited rescuer of God's people. He claims the anointing of the Lord, the holy one, in his mission to preach the good news to the poor—the poor in all senses of the word, including the poor in spirit. He will release (the same word used in the New Testament for 'forgive') the prisoners, those locked not only in physical prisons but also the emotional and spiritual chambers of bitterness, unforgiveness and despair.[31] He will bring sight to the blind, releasing both physical and spiritual sight so that people can glimpse the true, good and beautiful. He will set the oppressed free—all those downtrodden by persecution, systemic sin such as racism or classism, and discrimination. He will proclaim that now is the time of Jubilee, the moment for freedom, forgiveness and a fresh start.

Those assembled marvel at his words, but soon they wonder who speaks to them: he's Joseph's son, after all. Puzzlement leads to anger and fury when they question Jesus, and he warns them about their unbelieving ways. The stage is set for the work of the Son of God, the one who brings healing and salvation, but who also divides those who are receptive from those who are closed. As we see in the next section of Luke's Gospel, Jesus follows his pronouncement of his public ministry by healing the demon-possessed and the sick. He is a man not only of words but of action.

We who are familiar with Jesus don't always consider how radical he was and how upsetting he was to the status quo in religious circles when he lived. Though the religious teachers had been waiting for a messiah, they weren't expecting someone like Jesus. Instead of humbling themselves, being willing to be stretched and pushed out of their long-held expectations, they hardened their positions and rejected him. We see at the start of his public ministry that people will always react to Jesus in a polarised manner. Many will repent and welcome his kingdom; many, however, will not.

When we share the good news of Jesus, we too will meet with a mixture of responses. Some will want to know more, intrigued by his life and message, while others will think we're barmy, that we're committing ourselves to a myth of epic proportions. We shouldn't be surprised when people reject our invitation to hear more, for Jesus lived daily with people wanting to stone him for his claim of being the chosen one of God. But we who have received the gift of new life and freedom from our sins have to share his good news. It's just too good a gift to keep to ourselves.

## Prayer

*Lord Jesus Christ, you pronounced the good news of your kingdom that day in the synagogue to a mixed response. Though the people were intrigued, soon they became incensed. I too may meet this reaction when I share about how you've worked in my life, and I can become discouraged. But you, Lord, never gave in to such feelings. For you knew you were coming to save the lost, to redeem sinners, to impart freedom and joy and satisfaction in the hearts and minds of those who follow you. May I receive your gifts of love and peace this day, that I may be equipped to share your message with those whom I will meet. Prepare me even now with words that speak directly to their hearts, that your kingdom of heaven may be extended.*

## Monday

# Living water

When a Samaritan woman came to draw water, Jesus said to her, 'Will you give me a drink?'…

The Samaritan woman said to him, 'You are a Jew and I am a Samaritan woman. How can you ask me for a drink?'…

Jesus answered her, 'If you knew the gift of God and who it is that asks you for a drink, you would have asked him and he would have given you living water.'

'Sir,' the woman said, 'you have nothing to draw with and the well is deep. Where can you get this living water? Are you greater than our father Jacob, who gave us the well and drank from it himself, as did also his sons and his livestock?'

Jesus answered, 'Everyone who drinks this water will be thirsty again, but whoever drinks the water I give them will never thirst. Indeed, the water I give them will become in them a spring of water welling up to eternal life.'

The woman said to him, 'Sir, give me this water so that I won't get thirsty and have to keep coming here to draw water.'

He told her, 'Go, call your husband and come back.'

'I have no husband,' she replied.

Jesus said to her, 'You are right when you say you have no husband. The fact is, you have had five husbands, and the man you now have is not your husband. What you have just said is quite true.'

JOHN 4:7, 9–18, ABRIDGED

It seems incongruous that I felt so thirsty in the Boundary Waters Canoe Area of northern Minnesota, as it is filled with lake after lake of fresh water. But we were in the midst of a nine-mile portage—with canoes—in the middle of the night and had run down our water supplies. We knew we'd have no more fresh water until we reached our destination in the morning. When the thirst became too much, we ignored our shame (and good sense) and scooped up some of the stagnant water we found in puddles along the trail. A few hours later, reaching running water struck joy in our hearts.

We see another person seeking water in Jesus' interaction with the Samaritan woman at Jacob's well at the height of the day. Social convention doesn't keep Jesus from asking this woman for water. A single man on his own, especially a rabbi, would never talk to a woman on her own in his culture. Yet he breaks all of the rules of that society in his mission to share the promise of new life.

As they talk, the Samaritan woman misses the meaning of his statements. While he points her to eternal realities, she keeps asking about the stuff of the everyday. 'What is this water?' she asks, requesting it from Jesus so that she won't have to keep returning to the well. He tries to convey to her that he is a well of unending proportions, for he is the source of living water. From him comes water that flows clear and clean, bringing life and slaking thirst.

Only when he tells her 'everything I've ever done', as she says to the previously estranged townspeople (4:29), does she realise that he is special, a prophet. She no longer has to hide the fact of her life of sin, for Jesus sees her for who she is and accepts her. She who had been rejected and maligned is now known and loved. The living water he speaks of washes her clean, cleansing her from her wrongdoing as she accepts the gift of it. She who sneaked off to the well in the middle of the day—probably to avoid the sneers of the women who abhorred her—receives the forgiveness of her sins through the healing gift of living water.

This living water flows today, through God's Spirit and Jesus who lives within us. When we accept Jesus' invitation to follow him, he showers us with his love, cleansing us of our shameful actions. Not only do we receive his living water when we first become disciples, but it's there for us to dip into—or jump into—daily. We find no droughts in the kingdom of God, but rather an oasis of love, life, greenery and fruit.

Why not stop at Jesus' well today?

## Prayer

*Jesus, healer and releaser, forgive my sins.*
*Jesus, source of living water, slake my thirst.*
*Jesus, well of unending love, fill my heart.*

# Tuesday

# Forgiveness is healing

A few days later, when Jesus again entered Capernaum, the people heard that he had come home. They gathered in such large numbers that there was no room left, not even outside the door, and he preached the word to them. Some men came, bringing to him a paralysed man, carried by four of them. Since they could not get him to Jesus because of the crowd, they made an opening in the roof above Jesus by digging through it and then lowered the mat the man was lying on. When Jesus saw their faith, he said to the paralysed man, 'Son, your sins are forgiven.'

Now some teachers of the law were sitting there, thinking to themselves, 'Why does this fellow talk like that? He's blaspheming! Who can forgive sins but God alone?'

Immediately Jesus knew in his spirit that this was what they were thinking in their hearts, and he said to them, 'Why are you thinking these things? Which is easier: to say to this paralysed man, "Your sins are forgiven," or to say, "Get up, take your mat and walk"? But I want you to know that the Son of Man has authority on earth to forgive sins.' So he said to the man, 'I tell you, get up, take your mat and go home.' He got up, took his mat and walked out in full view of them all. This amazed everyone and they praised God, saying, 'We have never seen anything like this!'

MARK 2:1–12

Forgiveness is healing,[32] a finding that those in the medical profession have studied and documented. We may hear amazing stories of physical healing after someone has extended forgiveness to another, but more common forms can come through this act of grace as well. After all, when we are wracked with bitterness, we are more likely to be agitated and anxious. This increases the rate of our breathing and heightens the level of our adrenaline, which can be bad for our immune system. But when we forgive, we can experience lowered blood pressure, less depression and anxiety, and better sleep.[33]

As we see in Mark's Gospel, Jesus came to usher in the kingdom of heaven through the forgiveness of sins, including through this healing, which also shows the power of the love of one's friends. Jesus doesn't shy away from a confrontation with the teachers of the law in fulfilling his mission. When teaching in Capernaum, he responds to the great faith of these four friends of a paralysed man when he pronounces that the man's sins are forgiven. As we have seen, in the Hebrew scriptures the only source of forgiveness is God, so the Jewish teachers of the law immediately wonder what Jesus can mean by this statement. He must be a deluded blasphemer, they think, if he says he can forgive sins.

But Jesus, displaying his divine nature when he senses their thoughts, silences them not only with his words but with his actions. The Son of Man forgives sins, he says as he directs the man to walk out the door, healed. The man obeys, forgiven and free, while the teachers of the law remain imprisoned in their unbelief.

In speaking of healing, I don't want to imply that anyone who suffers physical ailments must have sinned. If that were true, we'd all be flat on our backs, wracked with pain. We just don't understand why some people are healed and others are paralysed or live with incurable and life-hampering illnesses. We hope, we pray and we believe in God's healing purposes, all the while acknowledging the mystery that the Lord heals some people while others don't enjoy the same level of healing this side of heaven. With those others, we ache and pray.

With that qualification, I want to encourage us all to ask the Lord to help us forgive the big and the small sins committed against us, for when we harbour anger and bitterness, not only are our emotions affected but our physical nature as well. When we release those who have hurt us, we too are released. And sometimes, in forgiving, we may receive freedom from the physical ailments we suffer. The great physician works in and through us for our good and his glory.

## Prayer

*Father God, you are the source of forgiveness and healing. I don't under-stand why many of those whom I love suffer, or why I myself sometimes endure pain and hardship. But I believe that you are good, that you love me, and that you want me to live in peace and joy, unhindered to serve you. Yet in our fallen world, where sin and disease have changed the default setting, I now can't escape being hurt and experiencing pain. Lord, into my places of wounding I ask you to come, that you might relieve my hurts and bring me closer to you. Bring renewal and new life to the very cells in my body; may you forgive so that I may be free.*

# Wednesday

# Heaping grace

'You have heard that it was said, "Eye for eye, and tooth for tooth." But I tell you, do not resist an evil person. If anyone slaps you on the right cheek, turn to them the other cheek also. And if anyone wants to sue you and take your shirt, hand over your coat as well. If anyone forces you to go one mile, go with them two miles. Give to the one who asks you, and do not turn away from the one who wants to borrow from you.

'You have heard that it was said, "Love your neighbour and hate your enemy." But I tell you, love your enemies and pray for those who persecute you, that you may be children of your Father in heaven. He causes his sun to rise on the evil and the good, and sends rain on the righteous and the unrighteous. If you love those who love you, what reward will you get? Are not even the tax collectors doing that? And if you greet only your own people, what are you doing more than others? Do not even pagans do that? Be perfect, therefore, as your heavenly Father is perfect.'

MATTHEW 5:38–48

'He got a biscuit, so I should get one too!'

Children often see things in stark terms, especially when they believe their rights are being impinged on or restricted. Those caring for them may soon tire of their eagle eyes and interpretation of what's fair. The concept of grace over law can feel foreign to these little ones whom we love, as it may have seemed for the people in Jesus' day.

We don't go far into Matthew's Gospel before reaching the Sermon on the Mount, the three-chapter discourse of Jesus in which he teaches his disciples on a mountain, for Matthew wants to convey Jesus' teachings as a means of carrying out his great commission to share the good news. And what enriching teaching we find here, for Jesus extends an invitation to life in the kingdom of God, a place where heaven descends to earth and we can enjoy and share the riches of God's love.

In the sermon, Jesus teaches specifically on forgiveness when he instructs the disciples on how to pray. He gives them what we know as the Lord's Prayer (which we'll look at tomorrow), but before then he shares the Beatitudes—words of blessing—and a series of statements that interpret the wisdom of the law in the Old Testament, several of which we'll examine that imply reconciliation.

We might think the phrase an 'eye for eye, and tooth for tooth' sounds retaliatory, but, as we dig into the cultural and historical setting in which it was spoken, we can see what's behind the statement and better understand Jesus' enlargement of it.[34] In the ancient Near East, this law of revenge, in contrast to what we might think it entails, was intended to *limit* retaliation, for punishments were often handed out that far exceeded the nature of the crime. Also, the law was to be applied by those in authority, not by individuals, and didn't have to be carried out for each and every offence. But by the time of Jesus, people were applying this law in their own disputes for the purpose of revenge.

Jesus, in contrast, wants to promote life and reconciliation and instructs his listeners not to look to enforcing the letter of the law. His command to 'turn to them the other cheek' may sound confusing to us, but a slap on the right cheek would have been done with the back of the right hand, implying more of an insult than injury. They are to submit to being insulted if that prevents an escalation of emotions and conflict. The instruction to go the second mile, too, heaps grace on the other person. Roman soldiers could require civilians to carry their load for a mile, so Jesus says, don't only go the required mile, but walk an extra mile as a gift.

What about 'Love your neighbour and hate your enemy'? Jesus expands that statement in mindblowing ways for those he addresses, sharing God's desire that all would be redeemed as they come to know and love him. When we love and pray for our enemies, we can't help but change the way we view them. We start to understand that they too are made in God's image, and we sense God's heart-longing that they would return to him. Through the Holy Spirit dwelling within, and through exercising wisdom, we can seek reconciliation with our enemies.[35]

We're over halfway through Lent.[36] How are you doing? How can you put Jesus' instructions into practice as you seek to live a life of love?

## Prayer

*Lord Jesus Christ, you loved your enemies and prayed for them, asking your Father to forgive them as they nailed you to a tree. That kind of love changes everything, and I'm in awe of it. Enfold me in this forgiving love so that I can extend it not only to my family and friends, but to those whom I find difficult and those who have hurt me. May I know the joy of loving the hard person, as helped by your Spirit within. Use me to bless others this day.*

# Thursday

# How to pray

'This, then, is how you should pray:

"Our Father in heaven,
hallowed be your name,
your kingdom come,
your will be done,
    on earth as it is in heaven.
Give us today our daily bread.
And forgive us our debts,
    as we also have forgiven our debtors.
And lead us not into temptation,
    but deliver us from the evil one."

For if you forgive other people when they sin against you, your heavenly Father will also forgive you. But if you do not forgive others their sins, your Father will not forgive your sins.'

MATTHEW 6:9–15

'It was as though God stopped me mid-sentence and said, "R.T., do you know what you are asking? That means you are wanting me to forgive them and bless them."'[37] So says R.T. Kendall about a time when he yearned to draw closer to the Lord. He was stopped short by the thought of extending forgiveness, for he knew that to have intimacy with God he had to decide whether he truly wanted the Lord to forgive those who had wronged him. After all, it's one thing to consider this notion of forgiveness in the abstract, but something different when we have a concrete example to wrestle with—with all of the accompanying feelings of hurt and betrayal.

Yet if we pray this prayer that Jesus gives his disciples (as part of the Sermon on the Mount), we ask the Lord to forgive those who wrong us, just as he forgives us. Because we've been redeemed and forgiven, we have the grace to reach out with forgiveness to those who malign us. Many biblical commentators agree that our salvation isn't on the line if we don't forgive,[38] but when we don't, we end up being penalised by an unforgiving attitude.

I'm not immune to unforgiveness and this prison of bitterness. When many years ago a prayer partner and confidante betrayed me, I felt the blow like a punch to the stomach. Having trusted her with buried dreams and desires, I felt exposed and vulnerable when she turned from me. We parted ways after a tearful phone call, during which I extended forgiveness. But in the years that followed, whenever I saw her in the community I'd experience a flash of pain. I knew I was still holding on to some hurt and anger.

I didn't see her often, but one day, when a mutual friend mentioned her name, I felt that familiar sensation of unforgiveness and knew that I wanted the Lord to release me from it. After all, it was nine long years after the event. I asked my friend to pray with me, and when we prayed I expressed my desire for God to set me free. I didn't feel any great emotion of release, but was amazed to run into my former prayer partner the very next day—she whom I could go for years without seeing. And this time when I saw her, I felt not pain but a desire that God would bless her. I didn't want to renew our friendship, but I no longer felt hurt. Thank God, I thought, for releasing me from these feelings of entrapment.

My example illustrates how fragile and tender we can be when we're hurt, and how long the process of forgiveness can be. I prayed the Lord's Prayer all those years while holding on to unforgiveness with this former friend, so did the Lord not forgive me? I can't say for sure—no one but the Lord knows—but I believe that God in his mercy forgave me even as he wished I would also extend his forgiveness. We are works in progress, needing his grace every day.

Might you be nursing feelings of being betrayed or wronged? If so, I pray that it wouldn't take nine years for you to be free, as it did for me. May the Lord soften your heart and loosen any chains that bind you, that you may experience release from this prison of pain.

## Prayer

*Father, Son and Holy Spirit, I need your grace and love even to consider forgiving those who have wronged me. I might assume that, in forgiving, I'll excuse their sins or not acknowledge the great pain they have caused me. But I know that you are the judge, and I want to leave the consequences in your hands. Remove from me the need to retaliate, and take the deep feelings of pain that I feel at their actions. I ask for the gift of total forgiveness, that I could love you with my whole heart, soul and mind as I love my neighbour as myself. Forgive me my sins, Lord, as I forgive those who sin against me.*

# Friday

# Love poured out

A woman in that town who lived a sinful life learned that Jesus was eating at the Pharisee's house, so she came there with an alabaster jar of perfume. As she stood behind him at his feet weeping, she began to wet his feet with her tears. Then she wiped them with her hair, kissed them and poured perfume on them.

When the Pharisee who had invited him saw this, he said to himself, 'If this man were a prophet, he would know who is touching him and what kind of woman she is—that she is a sinner.'

Jesus answered him, 'Simon, I have something to tell you.'

'Tell me, teacher,' he said.

'Two people owed money to a certain money-lender. One owed him five hundred denarii, and the other fifty. Neither of them had the money to pay him back, so he forgave the debts of both. Now which of them will love him more?'

Simon replied, 'I suppose the one who had the bigger debt forgiven.'

'You have judged correctly,' Jesus said.

Then he turned towards the woman and said to Simon, 'Do you see this woman? I came into your house. You did not give me any water for my feet, but she wet my feet with her tears and wiped them with her hair. You did not give me a kiss, but this woman, from the time I entered, has not stopped kissing my feet. You did not put oil on my head, but she has poured perfume on my feet. Therefore, I tell you, her many sins have been forgiven—as her great love has shown. But whoever has been forgiven little loves little.'

Then Jesus said to her, 'Your sins are forgiven.'

LUKE 7:37–38, 40–48

One day changed Terri Roberts' life for ever. She and her husband Chuck were shocked to learn that their son, whom they had raised in a strong Christian home, had entered an Amish school and gunned down ten girls, killing five of them before taking his own life. The horrors of the days that followed the atrocity remain clear in her mind and heart, but an unexpected gift resulted as well—the forgiveness of the Amish community. Braving the glare of the media at her son's burial, members of the Amish community whose girls had been wounded and killed formed a circle around the Roberts family to shield them from the intrusive telescopic lenses.

Terri tells in her book *Forgiven* how an unlikely friendship grew between her and some of the Amish families, such as through her weekly visits to one of the profoundly disabled girls. The love they have shown her—as one who felt a parent's responsibility for the awful killings—has given her hope and healing. She who has been forgiven much loves much.[39]

We see great love and great forgiveness as Jesus commends a 'sinful woman' who appears at the dinner he shares with a Pharisee, Simon. She would have gained access to him because meals with important people were often held with the door open to the public, so that others as well as the invited guests could benefit from the teaching of the honoured guest. She enters and in tears anoints Jesus with expensive perfume—possibly costing as much as a year's wages. She pours out her love in liquid form, washing his feet with profound gratitude.[40]

Jesus knows that Simon objects to his being anointed by this so-called sinful woman, so he shares the story of the debts forgiven. Simon begrudgingly acknowledges that this woman loves deeply because she has been freed from her sins, but we don't see how he reacts when Jesus points out that she has welcomed him much more than Simon has, even though he is the guest at Simon's table.

Simon and the other guests are stunned when Jesus says that her sins are forgiven, for, as we've seen, in Jewish thought, only God can forgive sins. Jesus not only equates himself with God but ushers in a new kingdom of grace in which people can forgive others. This lavish love can be poured out by the sinful and those who see themselves as holy.

The story illustrates not only the deep love of the forgiven, but the hard-heartedness of one who thinks he doesn't need forgiveness. Take a few moments as you ponder the story, considering where you would place yourself on the spectrum between the forgiven woman and the righteous Pharisee.

## Prayer

*Lord Jesus, you wanted your love to reach not only the woman who loved much, but also the man with a tough exterior and great influence. Reveal to me if I've looked to my position in society for meaning and affirmation instead of finding them in you. I want to be free to bow down before you, pouring out my precious oil as I wash your feet with tears of love. Receive me, whatever the state of my heart and whatever sins I may have done. Transform me into your likeness, that I may spread your sweet fragrance.*

## Saturday

# The unforgiving servant

'Therefore, the kingdom of heaven is like a king who wanted to settle accounts with his servants. As he began the settlement, a man who owed him ten thousand bags of gold was brought to him. Since he was not able to pay, the master ordered that he and his wife and his children and all that he had be sold to repay the debt.

'At this the servant fell on his knees before him. "Be patient with me," he begged, "and I will pay back everything." The servant's master took pity on him, cancelled the debt and let him go.

'But when that servant went out, he found one of his fellow servants who owed him a hundred silver coins. He grabbed him and began to choke him. "Pay back what you owe me!" he demanded.

'His fellow servant fell to his knees and begged him, "Be patient with me, and I will pay it back."

'But he refused. Instead, he went off and had the man thrown into prison until he could pay the debt...

'Then the master called the servant in. "You wicked servant," he said, "I cancelled all that debt of yours because you begged me to. Shouldn't you have had mercy on your fellow servant just as I had on you?" In anger his master handed him over to the jailers to be tortured, until he should pay back all he owed.

'This is how my heavenly Father will treat each of you unless you forgive your brother or sister from your heart.'

MATTHEW 18:23–30, 32–35

An acclaimed biblical scholar is not someone I would imagine as harbouring thoughts of killing his stepfather. But in a commentary on Matthew's Gospel, Michael Wilkins shares how, when he was a soldier in Vietnam, he became obsessed with the thought of inflicting revenge on the man who had caused his family great pain when he was growing up. He vowed that he would 'make him pay' for what he had done to his family.[41]

When Michael later became a Christian, however, he put vengeful thoughts out of his mind. Yet one day, four years later, his stepfather reappeared in his life. While sitting together in their living-room, Michael said, 'I made a vow in Vietnam that the first time I saw you, I would kill you. Today is that day.' As he witnessed the sweat pour off the older man, he continued, 'But I know now that I'm no better a person than you. God has forgiven me. And if he can forgive a sinner like me, I can forgive you. I will not allow you to hurt my family again, so don't think that this is made out of weakness. Rather, I forgive you because I have been forgiven.'[42]

What a stunning response, fuelled with emotion and extending mercy while not excusing the sins of the past! This biblical commentator reveals his humility in the reflections that follow the story, sharing how surprised he was to have made this offer of forgiveness to his stepfather, while also knowing that it came out of his transformation in Christ. As he says:

> My vow had been the rash, irresponsible reaction of a deeply hurt, bitter young sinner. However, my ability later to forgive came from the eternal, loving act of grace in Jesus' sacrifice for my sin. I discovered that the key to forgiveness is to stop focusing on what others have done *to* us and focus instead on what Jesus has done *for* us.[43]

Michael's story illustrates the parable of the unforgiving servant, for this academic didn't want to resemble the servant who enjoyed the release of debts of several billion (roughly, in today's terms) but who wouldn't release the debts of another who only owed a few thousand. Jesus tells the parable after Peter asks him how many times one should forgive someone in the community. The Old Testament (in books such as Amos and Job) teaches that to forgive three times is enough to show mercy, so Peter goes above the requirement of the law with his suggestion of seven times. But Jesus, reiterating God's great love for his people, expands the answer of how many times one should forgive, to a number that seems limitless. Because God has forgiven our sins, we too should welcome the sinner back into the community and extend forgiveness to them.

The parable we've read today shows an opposite response to the lived-out parable of the 'sinful' woman that we read yesterday. Whereas she responds with tears and gifts, the servant in the parable shows no mercy. Rather than being transformed by God, this man hardens his heart and resists God's love. Jesus' pronouncement on his fate is stark, saying that the master hands him over to the jailers to be tortured, and that his listeners too will be treated this way by his heavenly Father unless they forgive their brothers and sisters from the heart.

In a day and age when we don't like to hear pronouncements of eternal torture, neither can we wish away the biblical text. It's for each of us to examine our own heart, trusting the Lord through his Spirit to reveal any hidden sins or vows of unforgiveness. Then if we are presented with a situation like that of the academic and his stepfather, we too can extend the gift of forgiveness.

## Prayer

*Lord Jesus Christ, you explode our categories of thought and belief. I may think I'm being gracious in forgiving seven times instead of the required three. But you tell me to forgive 77 times, because I have been forgiven so greatly. Help me to remember just how much I need your grace in my life, or soon I will become like the unforgiving servant, holding the wrongs of others over their heads while I ignore the great release from sins that you have bestowed on me. May I live out the grace you extend to me, that others might know your love through my life.*

# Spiritual exercises and questions for individual reflection and group discussion

## The well of forgiveness

You will need scissors, thin card, pens and tape; or a plastic water bottle or aluminium tin can.

During the middle of the day, Jesus showered the woman who had many husbands with living water. As she experienced, the well of forgiveness is deep.

Take some time and fashion a well. The act of creating the well is more important than what you end up with, for you can do so prayerfully as a means of asking the Lord to show you what you thirst for. One way to make a well is out of thin card, cutting a circle for the bottom and a rectangle for the sides which you'll tape around the circle. You can decorate the sides if you wish. Another way is to cut off the bottom third of a plastic water bottle and wrap it in paper, or use a tin can, again wrapping it in paper and decorating it as you wish.

While you cut and tape and create, think about Jesus as the living water who cleanses and washes us clean. Can you name what you thirst for? How can you bring those desires and longings to God? Spend some time in prayer, asking God through his Holy Spirit to reveal how he can slake your thirst.

## Praying the Lord's Prayer

We might find the Lord's Prayer so familiar that we don't engage with it purposefully. Today or this week, commit to praying through the sections of the prayer that Jesus taught his friends as you ask him to bring alive his words. We can break it into six sections:

- 'Our Father in heaven, hallowed be your name.' Praise the Lord for his wondrous works in your life, community and the world.
- 'Your kingdom come, your will be done on earth as in heaven.' Commit to God situations in the world such as war, refugees, corruption, the environment and so on, asking that he would intervene with his grace and peace.
- 'Give us today our daily bread.' Ask God for the provisions you need, not only physical but also emotional and spiritual.
- 'Forgive us our sins as we forgive those who sin against us.' Ask God to reveal to you any sins you need to repent of. Receive his forgiveness and extend it, as you are able, to those who have wronged you. Pray for forgiveness on a bigger scale, that centuries-old conflicts could be solved peaceably.
- 'Lead us not into temptation but deliver us from evil.' Ask God for protection against the evil one and his schemes, not only in relation to your personal requests but around the world.
- 'For the kingdom, the power, and the glory are yours, now and for ever.' These words don't appear in the New Testament account, but they are a good way of ending your time with praise and adoration.

## The power of scent

As an act of kindness, as you think about the lavish outpouring of love when the woman anointed Jesus' feet with perfume, consider to whom you can give a wonderfully scented gift, such as flowers, lotions or bath salts, fragrant herbs, or some cuttings that you've been growing in anticipation of summer. Who can you bless?

# Questions for reflection and discussion

- How did you feel, here in Week 4, to reach the stories of Jesus?
- The story of the woman at the well is so evocative, for feeling like an outcast is a common experience. In reading the story this week, what struck you? How can you welcome living water into your life?
- The Sermon on the Mount is something that can be studied, examined and lived, and yet we've only been able to devote a day to a small part of it. How do Jesus' words bring life? Do they seem radical to you? Why or why not?
- 'Forgive us our sins as we forgive those who sin against us.' Do you see any warning in this phrase? Why or why not?
- I suspect that at times we've all wanted to act like the unforgiving servant. If that's true for you, how did you overcome the feelings of not wanting to extend forgiveness?

## Week 5

# Empowered by the Spirit: The Early Church

We're here at the fifth week—just two weeks left until we reach Resurrection Sunday and the glory of Jesus being raised from the dead. He who died for us yet lives, and no longer does sin hold or define us.

To reserve Jesus' passion for Holy Week, we turn to the early church and see how God's Spirit, released in his followers at Pentecost, changed them, empowering them to preach the gospel of forgiveness of sins. Peter is a prime example of a Spirit-filled, forgiven man, for he who denied Jesus now stands at Pentecost to give his impassioned testimony. We see how through the Spirit we are empowered to live by God's love.

Stephen too loves as he testifies to God's grace and redemption, but he becomes the first martyr for his beliefs. And yet he follows the example of Jesus, who extended forgiveness to his killers moments before his death.

We move to Ananias and Barnabas, examples of people used by God in bringing the hated Saul to become one of the greatest proponents for the Christian faith. Paul is a living example of God's redeeming love. He writes letters to the early church, one of which we'll read as we see how in Christ we leave behind the old and embrace the new. We forgive because the Lord forgives us.

We then turn to three other letters to the early church: the one to the Hebrews, the one by James, and one of the apostle John's final letters. Each shows how forgiveness is a key part of our Christian life, and how it comes about through prayer, faith and love.

The Christians in the early church move forth boldly to proclaim the good news of Jesus for the forgiveness of sins. Empowered by Christ living within them, they extend an invitation for people to accept this gift of forgiveness and new life.

# Sunday

# 'Repent and receive!'

Then Peter stood up with the Eleven, raised his voice and addressed the crowd: 'Fellow Jews and all of you who live in Jerusalem, let me explain this to you; listen carefully to what I say. These people are not drunk, as you suppose. It's only nine in the morning! No, this is what was spoken by the prophet Joel:

'"In the last days, God says,
    I will pour out my Spirit on all people…
I will show wonders in the heavens above
    and signs on the earth below…
And everyone who calls
    on the name of the Lord will be saved.".…

'Therefore let all Israel be assured of this: God has made this Jesus, whom you crucified, both Lord and Messiah.'

When the people heard this, they were cut to the heart and said to Peter and the other apostles, 'Brothers, what shall we do?'

Peter replied, 'Repent and be baptised, every one of you, in the name of Jesus Christ for the forgiveness of your sins. And you will receive the gift of the Holy Spirit. The promise is for you and your children and for all who are far off—for all whom the Lord our God will call.'

With many other words he warned them; and he pleaded with them, 'Save yourselves from this corrupt generation.' Those who accepted his message were baptised, and about three thousand were added to their number that day.

ACTS 2:14–17A, 19A, 21, 36–41

The number of people Billy Graham has preached to is mind-boggling—some say as many as 215 million people in live audiences over 185 countries. We'll never know the true impact of his mission to tell of God's love and redemption around the world. He follows in a long line of people who have shared their testimony with others—the thousands and the few—going back to Peter on the day of Pentecost. (We'll look, by the way, at Peter's confession and commission during Holy Week.)

We can marvel at Peter, a changed man who denied Jesus under pressure, but now, filled with the Holy Spirit, stands in front of the crowds to deliver an impassioned testimony about God's plan of salvation. The Holy Spirit is poured out on the disciples, but those watching are incredulous, saying the men are drunk. Peter names their doubts and digs into the Old Testament prophecies to show how this event is the culmination of God's work and plan (do read the full account in Acts 2 if you have time).

When Peter explains that Jesus is the Lord and Messiah (and thus, the persecuted one has been wrongly killed), the crowds are cut to the heart, convicted of their wrongdoing. 'What can we do?' they ask. Simple, says Peter—repent and be baptised. Leave your old way of life and be associated with us. Receive the forgiveness of sins and the gift of new life in the Holy Spirit. This gift is for you and yours and for many others, for God wants to shower his love near and far. Save yourself, he continues, from this corrupt generation.

And they do, for more than 3000 people become believers that day and the church has never looked back. We rightly call Pentecost the birthday of the church because of this wonderful gift of the Spirit, with people turning to God as they welcomed him into their lives.

Note the role played by the forgiveness of sins at this crucial stage. It's perhaps so obvious to us that we overlook it, but we can't be the church if we're weighed down with our wrongdoings. We need the slate to be washed clean so that we can move forward in our commission to spread the news of God's love and redemption.

The fact that the good news spreads through the testimony of a man who denied Jesus merely eight weeks before gives us hope. Although we let God down, yet he can restore us. We utter irritated words, or we gossip or seek power or act jealously, or we behave in a host of other awful ways. And yet when we turn from our sins, seeking forgiveness through Jesus' freeing act on the cross, we can receive pardon and release. The cross is an alive place, for there we receive the love of our triune God.

Are you ready, like Peter, to give your testimony to a hurting world?

## Prayer

*Loving Father, saving Lord, convicting Spirit, thank you for the gift of the Holy Spirit at Pentecost that empowers me to be part of your church. I know that I fail, but you forgive me and restore me. You can use me powerfully, even as Peter witnessed to those gathered for the Feast of Weeks as he opened up the Hebrew scriptures and showed how you were at work. Help me always to be prepared to give an answer to those who ask me for the reason for my hope, doing so with gentleness and respect and keeping a clear conscience, so that any who speak maliciously against me may be ashamed of their slander.*[44]

## Monday

# Surprising forgiveness

'You stiff-necked people! Your hearts and ears are still uncircumcised. You are just like your ancestors: you always resist the Holy Spirit! Was there ever a prophet your ancestors did not persecute? They even killed those who predicted the coming of the Righteous One. And now you have betrayed and murdered him—you who have received the law that was given through angels but have not obeyed it.'

When the members of the Sanhedrin heard this, they were furious and gnashed their teeth at him. But Stephen, full of the Holy Spirit, looked up to heaven and saw the glory of God, and Jesus standing at the right hand of God. 'Look,' he said, 'I see heaven open and the Son of Man standing at the right hand of God.'

At this they covered their ears and, yelling at the top of their voices, they all rushed at him, dragged him out of the city and began to stone him. Meanwhile, the witnesses laid their coats at the feet of a young man named Saul.

While they were stoning him, Stephen prayed, 'Lord Jesus, receive my spirit.' Then he fell on his knees and cried out, 'Lord, do not hold this sin against them.' When he had said this, he fell asleep.

ACTS 7:51–60

'There has never been a time in Christian history when someone, somewhere, has not died rather than compromise with the powers of oppression, tyranny and unbelief,' said one of the clergy from Westminster Abbey in 1998 when the ten statues of 20th-century martyrs were unveiled before the Queen.[45] The martyrs chosen, including Dr Martin Luther King Jr and Dietrich Bonheoffer, represent each continent. They follow the example of the very first martyr for his faith, Stephen.

Stephen is called up before the Sanhedrin, the Jewish rulers, because of opposition to the good works he does in the name of Christ. Those who are jealous of him bring trumped-up charges against him as false witnesses, and to them he delivers an impassioned defence of his faith (in Acts 7, which you may like to read). He looks to five key Old Testament times and representative figures to show how God never leaves his people—Abraham, Joseph, Moses, David and Solomon.

His speech doesn't go down well with the Jewish rulers. Look at the vivid language that Luke employs as he describes their reaction: they are furious and gnash their teeth; they cover their ears and yell at the top of their voices; they rush at him and drag him out of the city as they begin to stone him. Their response seems animal-like, fuelled by an evil hatred of all the good that Stephen has been doing and the truth he speaks in their midst.

But Stephen, filled with the Spirit and previously described as having 'the face of an angel' (Acts 6:15), sees a vision of heaven opening and Jesus standing at the right hand of God—standing and not sitting perhaps because he is Stephen's witness. Stephen's murder parallels that of Jesus in several ways, not least the words he speaks: 'Lord Jesus, receive my spirit' (7:59) and 'Lord, do not hold this sin against them' (v. 60). Perhaps in this Stephen models himself on his master. He acts as a conduit of God's grace as he puts himself into the hands of his Lord and forgives those who are persecuting him.

This extension of forgiveness seems miraculous. As I've reflected on Stephen's gracious words just before he dies, I've considered other startling acts of forgiveness—for example, by people who forgive the murder of someone close to them. As I've read some of these accounts, I've noticed how many of them say that they were surprised to find themselves offering forgiveness.

One example is the story of Lyn and Mick Connolly, whose son was stabbed one day on a street in Liverpool simply because he was in the wrong place at the wrong time. Less than a day later, they told a press conference that they forgave their son's killers. Reflecting on that act of forgiveness later, Lyn said, 'Mick and I both just said, we forgive. I must admit as the words came out of my mouth, it was a surprise to me.'[46]

These public acts of forgiveness stand out because they are so riveting in the face of the heinous crimes against loved ones. But I'm guessing that the foundation for the act of forgiveness was laid many years previously, as the person committed their life to following Jesus and as they practised forgiveness on a more mundane, everyday level. When it came time to forgive on a huge scale, they acted almost without thinking, for it had become second nature to them.

May we too have the grace and strength to forgive, as we are forgiven.

## Prayer

*Lord Jesus Christ, I stand in awe of those who have relinquished their lives rather than change their beliefs, and for those who are able to forgive the horrible atrocities committed against them. May you bring comfort to all who suffer because of these acts of persecution and senseless crimes, and may you bring conviction in the hearts of those who harm others, that they would repent. You are the judge and law-giver, and when I am wronged I look to you for strength not to take judgement into my own hands. May your will be done on earth as it is in heaven.*

## Tuesday

# True disciple

The Lord told [Ananias], 'Go to the house of Judas on Straight Street and ask for a man from Tarsus named Saul, for he is praying...'

'Lord,' Ananias answered, 'I have heard many reports about this man and all the harm he has done to your holy people in Jerusalem. And he has come here with authority from the chief priests to arrest all who call on your name.'

But the Lord said to Ananias, 'Go! This man is my chosen instrument to proclaim my name to the Gentiles and their kings and to the people of Israel.'...

When [Saul] came to Jerusalem, he tried to join the disciples, but they were all afraid of him, not believing that he really was a disciple. But Barnabas took him and brought him to the apostles. He told them how Saul on his journey had seen the Lord and that the Lord had spoken to him, and how in Damascus he had preached fearlessly in the name of Jesus. So Saul stayed with them and moved about freely in Jerusalem, speaking boldly in the name of the Lord. He talked and debated with the Hellenistic Jews, but they tried to kill him. When the believers learned of this, they took him down to Caesarea and sent him off to Tarsus.

Then the church throughout Judea, Galilee and Samaria enjoyed a time of peace and was strengthened. Living in the fear of the Lord and encouraged by the Holy Spirit, it increased in numbers.

ACTS 9:11, 13–15, 26–31

From a terrorist to a leader of the church—impossible?

Yesterday we saw how Saul, one who breathed murderous threats against anyone who followed Jesus, was involved in the stoning of

Stephen (7:58). But then something miraculous happened as Jesus appeared to Saul on the road to Damascus and said that he was the one whom Saul was persecuting (9:1–9). Saul's conversion is understandably famous, for it was so unexpected, as much as for the first disciples as for us.

When the Lord appears to Ananias in a dream and instructs him to go to Saul, Ananias understandably opposes the idea. After all, from everything he's heard, he thinks that presenting himself to Saul will result in instant death. But he obeys the Lord and goes to Saul, laying his hands on the blind man and speaking words of love and peace as he welcomes the Holy Spirit to fill him. How moving that scene must have been. A representative of the very body of believers Saul has been persecuting embraces the murderer. Ananias extends love and forgiveness through the laying on of hands, after which scales fall from Saul's eyes and he can truly see.

We see in Paul's letter to the church at Galatia that he was in Arabia and Damascus for three years after his conversion (Galatians 1:13–20), which was probably a time when he was quiet before the Lord, learning through revelation. He returns to Jerusalem a changed man. After so long away, I wonder how he thought the church would receive him. Instead of welcoming him, they fear him, and humanly, who can blame them? After all, he had been their chief persecutor.

But Barnabas steps in as a witness to Saul's true and lasting conversion, and the disciples receive Saul as one of their own. They who witnessed the miracles of Jesus have the faith to believe that God can change even the most ardent crusader against them. And the church is never the same again as Paul fearlessly shares his faith with the Gentiles, pouring himself out for them so that they too might know the saving love of Jesus.

Notice too how the Lord confers on the church a time of peace, strengthening and growth in Acts 9:31. Those who obey the Lord in forgiving and accepting Saul receive God's blessings.

Ananias and Barnabas played a key role in reaching out to Saul. How different would our history and our Bible be, had they not had the courage, strength and will to embrace this former persecutor? As you consider their influence, see if any people spring to mind who have acted just as courageously. May we be God's vessels through which he furthers his kingdom.

## Prayer

*Lord Jesus Christ, you reached out to Saul and changed him for ever. No longer was he a murderer, but one redeemed from his life of misguided zeal. I'm amazed at how he changed his life completely when he accepted the gift of your Spirit, and I admire and honour the courage of two men who were willing to stand up for him as they obeyed your voice. May I receive your strength and perseverance to follow your call, even if what I sense you're saying seems outrageous. As I weigh the message, may I have wisdom and discernment in obeying you.*

# Wednesday

# Hidden in Christ

Since, then, you have been raised with Christ, set your hearts on things above, where Christ is, seated at the right hand of God. Set your minds on things above, not on earthly things. For you died, and your life is now hidden with Christ in God. When Christ, who is your life, appears, then you also will appear with him in glory.

Put to death, therefore, whatever belongs to your earthly nature: sexual immorality, impurity, lust, evil desires and greed, which is idolatry. Because of these, the wrath of God is coming. You used to walk in these ways, in the life you once lived. But now you must also rid yourselves of all such things as these: anger, rage, malice, slander, and filthy language from your lips. Do not lie to each other, since you have taken off your old self with its practices and have put on the new self, which is being renewed in knowledge in the image of its Creator. Here there is no Gentile or Jew, circumcised or uncircumcised, barbarian, Scythian, slave or free, but Christ is all, and is in all.

Therefore, as God's chosen people, holy and dearly loved, clothe yourselves with compassion, kindness, humility, gentleness and patience. Bear with each other and forgive one another if any of you has a grievance against someone. Forgive as the Lord forgave you. And over all these virtues put on love, which binds them all together in perfect unity.

COLOSSIANS 3:1–14

Those who speak and write about the spiritual disciplines are not immune to sin and pride. James Bryan Smith, in his excellent book *Hidden in Christ*, tells about his hurt and disappointment when he was overlooked by someone: 'For several weeks I carried the pain and disappointment in my heart in the form of unforgiveness and a cool anger.'[47] But the Spirit spoke to him gently and he began to see that the problem was not that he'd been overlooked, but his pride. He didn't want to admit that he was a 'creature who lives each day by mercy', but wanted to think that he was 'special and powerful and deserving of all the good things that happen to me'.[48]

He realised that his pride was blocking his way to the freedom Christ extends, for he knew that our 'master and model' Jesus humbled himself as he took the form of a servant, giving his 'very life as a visible demonstration of forgiveness and reconciliation'. He prayed for several months to be able to forgive, and one day he finally could, for he sensed the presence of Jesus standing with him, the one who is not only 'the model but also the means of forgiveness' through his sacrifice on the cross.[49]

Humbling ourselves isn't easy, but if we don't bow down before the Lord with contrite hearts, we won't enjoy the release that forgiveness brings. The apostle Paul writes often on living out the new life in Christ, for, as we saw yesterday, he made a complete change when he stopped persecuting Jesus to become his disciple. Here he writes to the church at Colosse, which was suffering a crisis of confidence, and outlines how they should live out of the new self.

Because their lives are hidden in Christ, Paul says they should rid themselves of the practices of the old self—not only behaviours such as sins of the flesh, but also the sins that come through one's words. As they put on the clothes of the Spirit while living out of their new self, they are to bear with one another and forgive each other: 'Forgive as the Lord forgave you' (v. 13). And as an outer covering, they are to put on love, which will bind them 'all together in perfect unity' (v. 14).

As we see in Paul's text, forgiveness is a key part of our life in Christ. We live in a fallen world, experiencing bad things that we need to release to God. People fail us, and we fail them. On our own, we are nothing. So without a robust practice of extending and receiving forgiveness, we will be left wearing the dusty rags of the beggar instead of sporting the purple robes of the beloved heir. What a wonderful gift, to be daughters and sons of the Lord!

## Prayer

*Lord Jesus, help me to set my heart and mind on things above, not on earthly things, for I've died, and my life is hidden in you. Help me to put to death all that belongs to my earthly nature—sexual immorality, lust, evil desires and greed, which is idolatry. I used to walk in these ways in the life I once lived. Help me rid myself of anger, rage, malice, slander, and filthy language from my lips. I've taken off my old self with its practices and have put on the new self, which is being renewed in knowledge in the image of its Creator. Here there is no division, for you are in all.*

*As one of your chosen people, holy and dearly loved, help me to clothe myself with compassion, kindness, gentleness and patience. I want to forgive those whom I have a grievance against. And over all of these virtues, help me to put on love, which binds them together in perfect unity.[50]*

# Thursday

# Hall of faith

Now faith is confidence in what we hope for and assurance about what we do not see. This is what the ancients were commended for...

By faith Abraham, when called to go to a place he would later receive as his inheritance, obeyed and went, even though he did not know where he was going... And by faith even Sarah, who was past childbearing age, was enabled to bear children because she considered him faithful who had made the promise...

By faith Jacob, when he was dying, blessed each of Joseph's sons, and worshipped as he leaned on the top of his staff.

By faith Joseph, when his end was near, spoke about the exodus of the Israelites from Egypt and gave instructions concerning the burial of his bones...

By faith Moses, when he had grown up, refused to be known as the son of Pharaoh's daughter. He chose to be ill-treated along with the people of God rather than to enjoy the fleeting pleasures of sin...

And what more shall I say? I do not have time to tell about Gideon, Barak, Samson and Jephthah, about David and Samuel and the prophets...

Therefore, since we are surrounded by such a great cloud of witnesses, let us throw off everything that hinders and the sin that so easily entangles. And let us run with perseverance the race marked out for us, fixing our eyes on Jesus, the pioneer and perfecter of faith. For the joy that was set before him he endured the cross, scorning its shame, and sat down at the right hand of the throne of God.

HEBREWS 11:1–2, 8, 11, 21–22, 24–25, 32; 12:1–2

As a friend came to terms with the abuse she had suffered from her mother, she realised that she wanted to change her name. No longer did she want to be defined by a woman who had caused so much pain and anguish in her life. Rather she sensed God's still small voice giving her a new name, and to him she wanted to respond. Changing her name was an important part of her journey of healing, for by doing so she could extend another layer of forgiveness to her mother. She held firmly to her faith in the Lord, that he would make strong her identity in him.

We see in the letter to the Hebrews a Christian hall of fame—the heroes who are commended for their faith, which is 'confidence in what we hope for and assurance about what we do not see' (v. 1). They are singled out for their acts of faith, such as Abraham leaving his country and becoming a foreigner in a strange land, or Sarah believing she would conceive. All are commended for great acts of faith.

And yet, and yet. As we've seen throughout this Lenten journey, our heroes of the faith are heroes only because they are forgiven. Abraham feared the king of Egypt and passed off Sarah as his sister. Sarah took matters into her own hands and looked to Hagar to bear the heir; later she laughed in the tent, not believing the angel's promise that in a year she would give birth to a son. Jacob stole his brother's birthright, while his son Joseph was a dreamer who lorded his favourite-son status over his brothers. Moses was a murderer who killed an Egyptian and didn't believe that God could speak through him. And so on.

Yet none of these sins and wrongdoings are listed here in the book of Hebrews. Our heroes have been forgiven, and no longer does the Lord hold their failures against them. Instead, he lauds their actions of faith, the ways they heard and obeyed him, living out the call to follow him.

I find this tremendously encouraging, for it's one thing to know that we are forgiven, but another to see a list that demonstrates that as far as the east is from the west, the Lord removes our transgressions from us (Psalm 103:12). We're no longer the 'supplanter' (Jacob), but 'one who wrestles with God' (Israel). We move from 'princess' (Sarai) to 'mother of nations' (Sarah), or from Simon to Peter, the 'rock'. The Lord changes our names, and we are no longer bound to our previous identity. We who are forgiven can live as God's beloved.

## Prayer

*Lord God, you see me as I am—my faults and my courage—and you celebrate my acts of faith, as I see in this book of the Bible. These saints welcomed what was promised from afar and exercised their faith, believing that what you said would come true. Help me too to exercise faith, knowing that you will never renege on your promises. Lord, may you bring your kingdom here on earth, that I might spread your light and life and joy far and wide. As I live inspired by the heroes of faith, may I go forth as your ambassador of grace.*

# Friday

# The prayer of faith

Is anyone among you in trouble? Let them pray. Is anyone happy? Let them sing songs of praise. Is anyone among you ill? Let them call the elders of the church to pray over them and anoint them with oil in the name of the Lord. And the prayer offered in faith will make the sick person well; the Lord will raise them up. If they have sinned, they will be forgiven. Therefore confess your sins to each other and pray for each other so that you may be healed. The prayer of a righteous person is powerful and effective.

Elijah was a human being, even as we are. He prayed earnestly that it would not rain, and it did not rain on the land for three and a half years. Again he prayed, and the heavens gave rain, and the earth produced its crops.

JAMES 5:13–18

At the turn of the 20th century, James Fraser gave up pursuing a classical music career in England to live among the people of the Lisu tribe in China and share his faith. He laboured there for years before he realised that he had been praying a general prayer for them to come to faith, but what he needed to do was to pray a definite prayer of faith. He wrote in a letter to his prayer team back home:

> By definite prayer I mean prayer… where a definite petition is offered up and definite faith exercised for its fulfilment… The very word 'definite' means 'with fixed limits'. We are often exhorted, and with reason, to ask great things of God. Yet there is a balance in all things, and we may go too far in this direction. It is possible 'to bite off', even in prayer, 'more than we can chew'…

> I have definitely asked the Lord for several hundred families of Lisu believers. There are upwards of two thousand Lisu families

in the Tantsah district. It might be said, 'Why do you not ask for a thousand?' I answer quite frankly, 'Because I have not faith for a thousand.' I believe the Lord has given me faith for more than one hundred families, but not for a thousand. So I accept the limits the Lord has, I believe, given me.[51]

Fraser kept persevering with the Lisu people after praying his definite prayer, believing that the Lord had received his request and would answer it. Only ten years later did he see the fruit of his labours, when several hundred Lisu families turned to Christ as their Saviour. He believed the breakthrough came because of this specific prayer of faith.

Prayer is a key component in forgiveness, for through it God loosens ties and gives people the grace to forgive and to receive forgiveness. We see in James' letter, which he wrote to Jewish Christians outside Jerusalem, this emphasis on a 'prayer offered in faith'. So instead of praying only generally that the Lord would bring peace to our lives, we can pray the specific prayer that Fraser writes of, bringing the various aspects of the situation that concerns us before the Lord and asking him to work his ways.

As we see in the passage from James' letter, we are to pray in all situations, whether we're in trouble, we're happy or ill, or if we've sinned. And God will answer, just as he did for Elijah, who although he was 'a human being, even as we are', the Lord answered his prayers and sent rain. Releasing the situation with the specific details also means that we can leave it with the Lord, and not keep fretting over it. We trust that he hears us.

As outlined in *Mountain Rain*, the biography of Fraser, this act of prayer takes faith and it entails waiting, and is not something that we enter into lightly. Nor are we God: we can't dictate his answers, and perhaps he will say 'no' or 'not yet' to our requests. Unanswered prayers help to shape us and mould us. We might also find later that we have been seeking the wrong thing.[52]

May the Lord increase our faith and help us to know how to pray specifically.

## Prayer

*Lord God, I want to come to you when I'm in trouble and when I'm happy. When I'm not well, I seek your presence. When I sin, please forgive and heal me. Increase my faith, that I may pray earnestly according to your will, believing that you will answer. Show me any situations that I should bring before you with a definite act of faith. Help me to place them at your feet and leave them there, knowing that you are wiser and stronger and more able to answer my pleas than I could ever imagine. Thank you for your grace, help and never-ending love.*

# Saturday

# Love one another

This is the message we have heard from him and declare to you: God is light; in him there is no darkness at all. If we claim to have fellowship with him and yet walk in the darkness, we lie and do not live out the truth. But if we walk in the light, as he is in the light, we have fellowship with one another, and the blood of Jesus, his Son, purifies us from all sin.

If we claim to be without sin, we deceive ourselves and the truth is not in us. If we confess our sins, he is faithful and just and will forgive us our sins and purify us from all unrighteousness. If we claim we have not sinned, we make him out to be a liar and his word is not in us.

My dear children, I write this to you so that you will not sin. But if anybody does sin, we have an advocate with the Father—Jesus Christ, the Righteous One. He is the atoning sacrifice for our sins, and not only for ours but also for the sins of the whole world.

1 JOHN 1:5—2:2

The biblical translator and commentator Jerome, who straddled the fourth and fifth centuries, tells how when the beloved disciple John became so weak that he could no longer preach, church members would carry him into the gatherings at Ephesus to hear a word of exhortation. Again and again he would say, 'Little children, love one another.' When his listeners grew weary of the same message, asking him why he kept repeating it, he would say, 'Because it is the Lord's command, and if this is all you do, it is enough.'[53]

John loved the churches he oversaw, writing his three letters out of concern over the conflict in which they were immersed. Some of the people were denying that Jesus came to earth in bodily form, saying instead that he was a spirit. They also claimed that his death on the cross didn't atone for sin. With this background, we can see John's passion that the church should return to the truth of Jesus' bodily death and resurrection as the means of freeing them from their sins. In a series of dense statements rich with truth, he states forcefully the central tenets of the gospel: 'The blood of Jesus, his Son, purifies us from all sin' (1:7); 'If we confess our sins, he is faithful and just and will forgive us our sins and purify us from all unrighteousness' (v. 9); Jesus Christ 'is the atoning sacrifice' (2:2).

The cross is alive because of the death of the Son, through which God forgives our sins. There we receive freedom and hope; there we are given release and renewal. There we find our true selves as we shed our old selves and live out of the new. There, because we receive forgiveness, we too can forgive.

And it all comes back to love, as we see in the ageing John's message. The message may seem simple but it can be summed up in a well-known children's song written by Anna Bartlett Warner in 1860 that has theology robust enough to impress the most learned:

*Jesus loves me! This I know,*
*For the Bible tells me so;*
*Little ones to Him belong;*
*They are weak, but He is strong.*

Anna wrote this as part of a three-verse poem, but no longer are the latter verses sung regularly. They brim with the story of our Saviour's gift of freedom and our response:

*Jesus loves me! He who died*
*Heaven's gate to open wide,*
*He will wash away my sin,*
*Let His little child come in.*

*Jesus loves me! He will stay*
*Close beside me all the way;*
*Thou hast bled and died for me,*
*I will henceforth live for Thee.*[54]

As we ponder the message of John to those in the early church, we see it focusing on Jesus and on love, which is a profound and freeing message to consider as we move to Holy Week tomorrow. 'Little children, love one another.'

## Prayer

*Lord Jesus Christ, I'm often swayed away from your truth. Help me to know you more deeply through your revelation in the Bible and by your Holy Spirit so that I may not follow false gods. I seek your help so that love may define my life, for I know that because I am loved, I love. Because I am forgiven, I can forgive. Help me to love the people I encounter this day.*

# Spiritual exercises and questions for individual reflection and group discussion

## Drinking in the Holy Spirit

You will need a glass of water.

This is a simple but profound exercise to undertake as we think about Pentecost and the freedom that comes from the Holy Spirit living within us. As you pour a glass of water, consider part of Paul's letter to the church at Corinth: 'For we were all baptised by one Spirit so as to form one body—whether Jews or Gentiles, slave or free—and we were all given the one Spirit to drink' (1 Corinthians 12:13). Ponder each section of the verse. If you are able to ask for a fresh infilling of the Holy Spirit, do so as you drink the water. Receive the Spirit into your body even as you receive the water.

## Stones

You will need a collection of stones.

Stones became a murderous weapon when the crowd turned on Stephen after he had testified to how the Lord worked in and through his people. Stones also have a positive connotation in the Bible: for example, Jesus is called the cornerstone (Ephesians 2:20) and the members of the church are living stones (1 Peter 2:5).

Examine the stones you've chosen for this exercise, holding them and feeling their weight. When you think of the stones used against Stephen, pray for those who are persecuted in the name of Christ around the world, suffering for their faith. Thinking of the living stones, pray for fellow Christians you know who need encouragement and support. Considering the cornerstone, give thanks to the Father for sending his Son on whom to build his church.

# Blindness

You will need a scarf.

When we think about Saul's conversion, we don't often consider that he was blind for three days. He who was so sure of his vision of God could then see nothing. What did he experience during that time? What was he feeling and thinking?

Tie a scarf around your eyes and spend some time in prayer. Note what feelings you experience. Do you feel fearful? Vulnerable? How do your prayers change because of the physical lack of sight?

Pray that the Lord would reveal anything in your life that may be keeping you from seeing what is true, good and beautiful.

# Questions for reflection and discussion

- Consider Peter's call on the day of Pentecost: 'Repent and be baptised, every one of you, in the name of Jesus Christ for the forgiveness of sins. And you will receive the gift of the Holy Spirit' (Acts 2:38). How could you issue a similar call today in ways that would be appropriate for those to whom you speak?
- How can you build daily acts of forgiveness into your life? What do you think of my musing on Monday about how these little acts can build up to a big act of faith during a time of crisis?
- Have you thought about being hidden in Christ, as we saw in Colossians 3? What does this mean for you?

- Who would be your heroes of the faith? They could be people you've known or people you've read about from history. How do they inspire you?

- What do you think of a specific prayer of faith as opposed to a general prayer (such as the one that James Fraser prayed)? Is this something you have implemented, or will implement, in your own life?

## Holy Week

# Forgiveness Enacted: The Passion of Jesus

We've reached Holy Week, the week when we travel with Jesus through the momentous events that lead us to the cross. I invite you to join me in considering, day by day and throughout the week, the events that Jesus experienced. In the spiritual exercises that follow the week's readings, I've listed these events in order so that we can reflect on them together. It's a profound way to practise the presence of Jesus as we invite him into our daily lives by considering what he experienced during his last week on earth.

We start with Palm Sunday and Jesus riding into Jerusalem in triumph—but on a donkey. Clearly this is no ordinary king. We then examine some of Jesus' parables, both lived-out and shared by him, including his forgiveness of the woman caught in adultery and the parable of the lost son (which could also be called the story of the forgiving father).

Then we move into the events that start on Maundy Thursday, examining some of Jesus' teaching of the disciples at their last supper together. Then come the sombre events of Good Friday and the waiting on Holy Saturday.

And then at last, we reach the pinnacle of our journey, the start of the Easter season—Resurrection Sunday. And together we raise our voices in joy, saying, 'Alleluia! Christ is risen! He is risen indeed! Alleluia!'

## Palm Sunday

# The coming king

As they approached Jerusalem and came to Bethphage on the Mount of Olives, Jesus sent two disciples, saying to them, 'Go to the village ahead of you, and at once you will find a donkey tied there, with her colt by her. Untie them and bring them to me. If anyone says anything to you, say that the Lord needs them, and he will send them right away.'

This took place to fulfil what was spoken through the prophet:

'Say to Daughter Zion,
    "See, your king comes to you,
gentle and riding on a donkey,
    and on a colt, the foal of a donkey."'

The disciples went and did as Jesus had instructed them. They brought the donkey and the colt and placed their cloaks on them for Jesus to sit on. A very large crowd spread their cloaks on the road, while others cut branches from the trees and spread them on the road. The crowds that went ahead of him and those that followed shouted,

'Hosanna to the Son of David!'
'Blessed is he who comes in the name of the Lord!'
'Hosanna in the highest heaven!'

When Jesus entered Jerusalem, the whole city was stirred and asked, 'Who is this?'

The crowds answered, 'This is Jesus, the prophet from Nazareth in Galilee.'

MATTHEW 21:1–11

'All of life is Lent.' So I said to a visiting American friend not long after I had moved to England, for although I adored being married to my new husband, I felt as if I had lost so much in the move to a new country—job, family and friends, familiar customs and language. I had tried to observe my usual practice of various fasts during Lent but gave up after a few days when it all felt so hard, my heart hurting from the accumulated losses.

After a few years, however, I settled in, finding I could open my mouth without uttering too many gaffes and making some treasured friends who accepted me as I was. I started to think again about observing Lent with some spiritual practices, for I remembered how much richer Holy Week and Resurrection Sunday had been when I had prepared myself during Lent.[55]

Here we are at Palm Sunday, marking the start of Holy Week. Jesus knows it is time to fulfil prophecies in the Hebrew scriptures such as Zechariah 9:9: 'Your king comes to you… lowly and riding on a donkey.' By riding a donkey, a king signifies that he comes in peace and not as a military leader. Also, Matthew is the only one of the four Gospel writers to include the detail that the disciples bring both a donkey and a young colt, for he wants to refer to the Old Testament prophecy of Zechariah. It was customary to have the mother of the unbroken animal next to it when it was first ridden to keep it under control.[56]

The crowd who have gathered to celebrate the festival of Passover yearn for the Messiah and so throw palm branches at his feet, shouting with joy and adoration. But what they expect is a political messiah, someone to stand for them against Rome. They cannot guess that their cries of adulation at the beginning of the week will turn to the mocking taunts of 'Crucify him!' at the end.

Jesus isn't the one whom people expect him to be. The Messiah was born a baby in humble circumstances, not a palace. He preaches a message of salvation for those who repent and believe. He heals the sick and those possessed by demons, and even raises several from the dead. And now he will perform his greatest act of love and mercy, by dying on the cross so that God's people can come to him unhindered by their sins.

Whether or not you've observed Lent as you might have wished to at the start, consider how you can devote yourself to the triune God this Holy Week. Today you might want to read the above passage imaginatively, putting yourself into the story—perhaps as the disciple finding the donkey and colt for Jesus, or maybe as a member of the crowd.[57] Ask the Lord to show you what might be the best spiritual practices suited just to your passions, personality and needs. I trust he'll answer your request magnificently.

## Prayer

*Lord Jesus Christ, you came and blew away everyone's expectations of what the King of kings and Lord of lords would look like. As we enter into the events of this Holy Week, I come to you in humility, bowing myself before you, confessing my sins and receiving your forgiveness. May the events of this last week of your life be brought alive in my imagination, that I might know you more intimately and be more grateful for your sacrifice, which gives me life. I join the crowds to shout out with joy, 'Hosanna to the King of kings! Blessed are you who comes in the name of the Lord! Hosanna in the highest heaven!'*

# Monday

# Bought by love

At dawn he appeared again in the temple courts, where all the people gathered round him, and he sat down to teach them. The teachers of the law and the Pharisees brought in a woman caught in adultery. They made her stand before the group and said to Jesus, 'Teacher, this woman was caught in the act of adultery. In the Law Moses commanded us to stone such women. Now what do you say?' They were using this question as a trap, in order to have a basis for accusing him.

But Jesus bent down and started to write on the ground with his finger. When they kept on questioning him, he straightened up and said to them, 'Let any one of you who is without sin be the first to throw a stone at her.' Again he stooped down and wrote on the ground.

At this, those who heard began to go away one at a time, the older ones first, until only Jesus was left, with the woman still standing there. Jesus straightened up and asked her, 'Woman, where are they? Has no one condemned you?'

'No one, sir,' she said.

'Then neither do I condemn you,' Jesus declared. 'Go now and leave your life of sin.'

JOHN 8:2–11

Jean Valjean's life was changed by grace. Though he stole from a bishop who had shown him hospitality, he received forgiveness from this bishop instead of condemnation. When the police questioned the cleric, he told them that Jean Valjean not only owned the pieces of silver, but that he had forgotten to take the candlesticks as well. When he was leaving, the bishop whispered to him, 'Jean Valjean, my brother, you no longer belong to evil, but to good. It is your soul I am buying for you; I withdraw it from dark thoughts and from the spirit of perdition, and I give it to God.'[58] No longer did he belong to evil, for although he was a social outcast because he was a convicted criminal, yet he changed his life to embody grace and goodness.

Victor Hugo's novel illustrates the power of forgiveness to change lives. We see this power in the Gospel story we read today. Although we don't know what happened to the woman after Jesus had freed her, and whether her life was marked by grace and gratitude, we can hope that she left her life of sin. The story exemplifies how Jesus forgives as he stands up to the teachers of the law who are out for justice.

I should mention that some find this biblical text troubling, for it wasn't included in the early manuscripts of the Bible. But many biblical scholars believe that it may have been part of Luke's Gospel, and most are happy to include it as part of the biblical canon.[59] In fact, some biblical commentators wonder if the story was left out of early Greek manuscripts because the subject was sexual sin, with the 'sinner' in question a woman, and Jesus' grace-filled response to her seemed too provocative to the early church.[60]

Jesus doesn't fall into the trap set by the teachers of the law when they bring to him a woman caught in adultery. We can tell by their language that they are bringing forth a legal claim: they have caught her in the act and they want her punished publicly, which will result in her death. But Jesus isn't interested in legalistic punishment, especially as we only see the woman accused and not the man who has committed adultery with her. We don't know what Jesus wrote in the sand, but he turns the tables on the accusers when he highlights their own sinful hearts. As each of them realises how they have sinned, they drop their stones and walk away. And although Jesus didn't condemn the woman, neither does he excuse her actions, saying that she should no longer live a life of sin.

Our freedom and forgiveness come from the death of Jesus on the cross. There, the most heinous of crimes can be forgiven, as well as the everyday pettiness we indulge in. Jesus died so that the Judge wouldn't hear the accusers' case as they lay out the evidence against us. Rather, he stands in as our Advocate, pleading our innocence because of his action on the cross.

It's enough to make us, like Jean Valjean, receive the silver candlesticks with gratitude as we ask God to help us leave our lives of sin.

## Prayer

*Father God, you sent your Son to save me, and your Spirit to convict me. May I turn from my evil ways, whether of adultery, gossip, lies, bitterness, stealing, or whatever else keeps me from you. Forgive me for the big sins and the small. I deserve the stones and the handcuffs, but you grant me mercy. May I extend the same mercy to those who wrong me. And may you bring peace and healing between people who are at war with each other, whether in villages or nations. We need your grace and forgiveness; we yearn for your love and peace, in the name of Christ.*

# Tuesday

# The found son

Jesus continued: 'There was a man who had two sons. The younger one said to his father, "Father, give me my share of the estate." So he divided his property between them.

'Not long after that, the younger son got together all he had, set off for a distant country and there squandered his wealth in wild living…

'But while he was still a long way off, his father saw him and was filled with compassion for him; he ran to his son, threw his arms round him and kissed him.

'The son said to him, "Father, I have sinned against heaven and against you. I am no longer worthy to be called your son."

'But the father said to his servants, "Quick! Bring the best robe and put it on him. Put a ring on his finger and sandals on his feet. Bring the fattened calf and kill it. Let's have a feast and celebrate. For this son of mine was dead and is alive again; he was lost and is found." So they began to celebrate…

'The elder brother became angry and refused to go in. So his father went out and pleaded with him…

'"My son," the father said, "you are always with me, and everything I have is yours. But we had to celebrate and be glad, because this brother of yours was dead and is alive again; he was lost and is found."'

LUKE 15:11–13, 20–24, 28, 31–32

The parable of the lost son (or prodigal son) can be so familiar that we lose the sense of scandalous grace that it represents. Sometimes, however, the impact returns in an instant, as happened when I was leading a spiritual exercise with a group of women. I read the parable out, but I substituted a lost 'daughter' and a corresponding older sister. One of the women listening became emotional as the story struck home. The Spirit was at work in her life and in the life of her family.

Jesus tells the parable as the culmination of three stories about lost things being found: the lost sheep and the lost coin come before the lost son. This is his longest parable (so long that I couldn't include the full text—do read the whole story if you're able, in Luke 15:11–32), filled with details that would have resonated with his listeners.

That a father would gather his robes, exposing his ankles and feet, to run towards his son was unthinkable in that day, especially as the father was a prominent man in the community. But he had counted his son as dead and welcomed him home with joy. His son's prepared speech of confession is tossed to one side: the father doesn't even let him finish but acknowledges him as a son, one to be celebrated and rejoiced over. Even though the son basically wished the father dead when he demanded his portion of the inheritance, the father stretches out his hands and his heart.

But the older brother isn't pleased. He has been working out in the fields during the joyful reunion and returns to a party that he doesn't appear to be invited to. Expressing his disgust, he demands to know why his father would lavish the gift of a fattened calf on his brother when he hasn't even been able to enjoy a goat with his friends. His father's response is memorable for its grace and love: 'All I have is yours. Come, don't be angry, but rejoice! For your brother, whom we thought was dead, is alive!'

We don't see how the older brother responds in the story, but we know how the Pharisees reacted to Jesus: they prosecuted him and nailed him to a tree. Not everyone wants to receive God's scandalous grace.

But for those who have ears to hear and a heart ready to receive, they—yes, we—can accept the gift of forgiveness and new life. Even if we have squandered our inheritance, throwing it away on loose living and reckless spending, the Lord will welcome us back into his arms. If we harbour resentment against those who we think don't deserve to be part of the Christian family, the Lord wants to clear away the bitterness and disgust so that we can all be joyful members of his family.

During this Holy Week, as we consider Jesus' scandalous actions of grace and love poured out, place yourself into this parable through your imagination. Who are you? The younger child? The older sibling? The parent, longing for a loved one's return?

## Prayer

*Father of grace, of outstretched arms, my heart overflows with gratitude as I see you running towards me. I'm humbled and amazed that you would welcome me back home, even after I left you. I don't deserve your grace and forgiveness. Help me to live as one forgiven, who desires to further your kingdom on earth as your Spirit dwells within. Help me to remain grateful and not to become resentful when I hear of all the other members of the family whom you welcome back so lovingly. I know that you have no shortage of love. Thank you, loving Father.*

# Wednesday

# Hatred without reason

'If the world hates you, keep in mind that it hated me first. If you belonged to the world, it would love you as its own. As it is, you do not belong to the world, but I have chosen you out of the world. That is why the world hates you. Remember what I told you: "A servant is not greater than his master." If they persecuted me, they will persecute you also... Whoever hates me hates my Father as well. If I had not done among them the works no one else did, they would not be guilty of sin. As it is, they have seen, and yet they have hated both me and my Father. But this is to fulfil what is written in their Law: "They hated me without reason."

'When the Advocate comes, whom I will send to you from the Father—the Spirit of truth who goes out from the Father—he will testify about me...

'When he comes, he will prove the world to be in the wrong about sin and righteousness and judgement: about sin, because people do not believe in me; about righteousness, because I am going to the Father, where you can see me no longer; and about judgement, because the prince of this world now stands condemned.'

JOHN 15:18–20, 23–26; 16:8–11

As the phone rang in the middle of the night, Reverend David Triggs woke to the news that an arsonist had set his church on fire. Moments later, he arrived to see it blazing with flames, this the beloved place where he had led his church community to live and love as Christ's ambassadors. As he stood watching the firefighters battle the flames, he sensed God challenging him to forgive whoever had caused this heart-wrenching damage. He saw a vision of Jesus on the cross and remembered how Jesus forgave there. He said, 'Before I could utter a word to the firemen, to anyone, I had already found forgiveness for the person who did this. We preach that the core foundation of Jesus' ministry is forgiveness... We can't preach that on Sundays and not live it out.'[61]

Many African-American churches have been subjected to racially motivated attacks in America, not only the burning of buildings but horrible atrocities in which worshippers have been gunned down in their churches. They are examples of those who have suffered the persecution that Jesus speaks of with his disciples, in his Last (or Farewell) Discourse (John 14—17). After Jesus and his friends have eaten their last supper together, they walk from the upper room to the garden where Judas will betray him, and, on the way, Jesus teaches and prays for them.

He warns them not to be surprised when they are hated, for their master was hated first. But Jesus also promises—four times during this talk with the disciples—the coming Advocate, the Holy Spirit, who will not only bring comfort when people hate 'without reason' but will also convict the world over the sins committed. The word 'convict' has a legal connotation here, meaning that the Holy Spirit not only accuses people of their sin but also brings about a sense of guilt for the wrongdoing. As one biblical commentator puts it, 'The Spirit is the prosecuting attorney who presents God's case against humanity. He creates an inescapable awareness of sin' so that it cannot be evaded or dismissed by excuses.[62]

The Advocate convicts those sinning, and as we see in the example of the burning church, he convicts those who love him as well. The pastor, through the strength of the Spirit dwelling within him, offered forgiveness to the perpetrator of the crime even before the flames had been extinguished. The pastor wouldn't let flames of unforgiveness burn in his life, leaving destruction in their wake.

We may or may not suffer the persecution that these brothers and sisters in Christ endure, but we can embody forgiveness with the help of God when we are slighted or maligned or hurt. May we be people with malleable hearts who can extend an olive branch of peace.[63]

## Prayer

*Lord God, my heart hurts when I hear of atrocities committed against your people. I think of families ripped apart and lives changed because of the hatred some harbour against those who follow you. May you bring about justice, so that hatred would cease. May you pour your love and mercy on to those who are suffering, that they might find healing and release. May I be your agent of change, standing against such persecution whenever I come across it, to make your world a better place.*

## Maundy Thursday

# Broken for you

On the first day of the Festival of Unleavened Bread, the disciples came to Jesus and asked, 'Where do you want us to make preparations for you to eat the Passover?'

He replied, 'Go into the city to a certain man and tell him, "The Teacher says: my appointed time is near. I am going to celebrate the Passover with my disciples at your house."' So the disciples did as Jesus had directed them and prepared the Passover...

While they were eating, Jesus took bread, and when he had given thanks, he broke it and gave it to his disciples, saying, 'Take and eat; this is my body.'

Then he took a cup, and when he had given thanks, he gave it to them, saying, 'Drink from it, all of you. This is my blood of the covenant, which is poured out for many for the forgiveness of sins. I tell you, I will not drink from this fruit of the vine from now on until that day when I drink it new with you in my Father's kingdom.'

When they had sung a hymn, they went out to the Mount of Olives.

MATTHEW 26:17–19, 26–30

She hadn't wanted her husband to divorce her, but as they had been separated for five years she couldn't contest it. On the day when the divorce was being made final, she went back to the church where they had married. Wanting to be on her own and feeling annoyed when a midweek Communion service started, she mourned the loss of her husband. Then she felt the Lord ask her to take off her wedding ring as a way of marking the end of her marriage. 'Everything in me wanted to leave the ring where it was, but I also knew that peace only comes through obedience. An enormous surge of grief nearly choked me as I pulled it off and sat clutching it in my palm while the service progressed.'[64]

Jennifer walked up the aisle with everyone else to take Communion and knelt where she had once said her wedding vows. Again, she sensed the nudge of the Lord as he asked her, 'Will you give Tony to me—finally?' As a way of saying 'yes' she held out the ring on her hand when her turn came to receive the bread.

When she opened her eyes, she saw that the vicar had placed the wafer on top of her ring: 'All I could see was the cross on the white wafer. At that moment it felt as if Christ was covering our mess with his own dazzling white purity.'[65] She felt a rush of peace, forgiveness and release, and never again put on the ring. She sent it to her former husband as a way of releasing him to his new marriage.

Most times when we receive the Lord's Supper—or the Eucharist or Holy Communion, depending on what we call it—we don't experience such a profound depth of meaning. But this act of remembrance is a means by which God grants the forgiveness of sins. As we participate, we follow Jesus as he shares the Last Supper with his friends on the Jewish festival of Passover. He takes some ordinary bread and does something extraordinary with it, breaking it and giving it to them while saying that it is his body. Similarly he takes the cup of wine (which biblical scholars think was the third cup used during Passover, the cup of blessing) and gives it to his disciples while saying it is his blood, 'poured out for the forgiveness of sins'.

The apostle Paul wanted those in the early church to continue celebrating this act of blessing and remembrance, instructing them in how to share in it with pure hearts (see his corrections in 1 Corinthians 11:17–34, for instance). And, although Christians vary in the way they celebrate Communion, it has been, and continues to be, a unifying act in which we seek God's forgiveness for our sins.

Perhaps you are participating in a Seder meal with your church today, or using another way of marking Maundy Thursday, the day when we remember the Lord's last meal with his friends. Consider the bread of life, broken in two, and the cup of blessing, poured out in forgiveness of sins. How can you take into the world the blessings you receive?

## Prayer

*Lord Jesus Christ, I humble myself before you on this day when we remember your last hours. You have given the gift of new life and forgiveness through your broken body and poured-out blood. May I never take for granted what you have done and how it sets me free. You forgive me my sins, that I might share your love with my neighbours. I receive you and your gifts with a grateful heart.*

# Good Friday

# 'Father, forgive'

When they came to the place called the Skull, they crucified him there, along with the criminals—one on his right, the other on his left. Jesus said, 'Father, forgive them, for they do not know what they are doing.' And they divided up his clothes by casting lots.

The people stood watching, and the rulers even sneered at him. They said, 'He saved others; let him save himself if he is God's Messiah, the Chosen One.'

The soldiers also came up and mocked him. They offered him wine vinegar and said, 'If you are the king of the Jews, save yourself.'

There was a written notice above him, which read: THIS IS THE KING OF THE JEWS...

It was now about noon, and darkness came over the whole land until three in the afternoon, for the sun stopped shining. And the curtain of the temple was torn in two. Jesus called out with a loud voice, 'Father, into your hands I commit my spirit.' When he had said this, he breathed his last.

The centurion, seeing what had happened, praised God and said, 'Surely this was a righteous man.'

LUKE 23:33–38, 44–47

Darkness descends on the land as the sun stops shining. The curtain tears in two and Jesus breathes his last. Life will never be the same again.

On this holy day we remember with awe and wonder the death of our Lord and Saviour. He who could have been sitting at his Father's right hand in heaven came to earth to endure abuse of the worst kind. He looked at his persecutors with love and uttered words that would set them—and us—free: 'Father, forgive them; for they know not what they do' (v. 34, KJV).

Words seem lacking on a day that begs for silence and reflection, so I offer a poem based on the Gospel account:

*The suffering servant*
*Silent to their mocking*
*Their words fleeting*
*Your act remains*

*A kiss received*
*A kiss that betrays*
*From lips come lies*
*Rooted deep within*

*Before Pilate you stand*
*The battering shouts and jeers*
*From those seeking blood*
*And an end to your reign*

*A whip to your back*
*The bruising cross*
*Splinters and shame*
*You bear it all*

*In each palm a nail*
*The healing hands*
*Now bleeding and exposed*
*Sweat running through the gashes*

*Their words as weapons*
*For them you weep*
*Forgiving from the heart*
*Those pounding the nails*

*The last you breathe*
*Giving up your spirit*
*The darkness of death*
*No more the sun shines*

*They think they win*
*But human bonds too weak*
*A stone over your grave*
*Can never hinder your love*

## Prayer

*Lord Jesus Christ, Son of the living God, have mercy on me, a sinner. May my life reflect your forgiveness; may I extend your grace and mercy to those who wrong me; may I seek your cleansing when I turn from you. Come, Lord Jesus, and fill me afresh with your peace as I thank you for your sacrifice of love.*

## Holy Saturday

# Hopes dashed

Now there was a man named Joseph, a member of the Council, a good and upright man, who had not consented to their decision and action. He came from the Judean town of Arimathea, and he himself was waiting for the kingdom of God. Going to Pilate, he asked for Jesus' body. Then he took it down, wrapped it in linen cloth and placed it in a tomb cut in the rock, one in which no one had yet been laid. It was Preparation Day, and the Sabbath was about to begin.

The women who had come with Jesus from Galilee followed Joseph and saw the tomb and how his body was laid in it. Then they went home and prepared spices and perfumes. But they rested on the Sabbath in obedience to the commandment.

LUKE 23:50–56

For us, a day of waiting. We don't like to wait, whether for a friend to arrive for dinner or while standing in a queue at the supermarket. As society rushes forward with more technology to make things go even faster, we like to wait even less. But waiting is good for our souls, for as we pause we perhaps lean on the Lord a little bit more. We learn to shush the insistent voices inside that hurry us along. We seek to discern the still, small voice—with an emphasis on 'still'.

For those who love Jesus, a day of grief. They forget that Jesus will rise from the dead—as we see in Luke 24:6–8, when the angels speak to the women at the tomb: '"Remember how he told you, while he was still with you in Galilee: 'The Son of Man must be delivered over to the hands of sinners, be crucified and on the third day be raised again.'" Then they remembered his words.' The disciples aren't waiting but grieving. We can guess that they are disillusioned and stunned.

We don't have in the Gospels an account of what the disciples did on the sabbath, except that the women from Galilee rested 'in obedience to the commandment' (Luke 23:56). We do learn that on the Preparation Day, which was probably just before sundown on Friday, Joseph of Arimathea obtained permission from Pilate to take down Jesus' body and bury it in a new tomb. He wanted to obey the law as given in the Old Testament (see Deuteronomy 21:22–23).

Unlike the disciples, the chief priests and the Pharisees remember Jesus' statement that after three days he will rise again (as recounted in Matthew 27:62–66). When they go to Pilate on the day after Preparation Day to request that the tomb be made more secure, Pilate agrees, sending a guard. As we on the other side of the resurrection know, the Lord uses these persecutors of Jesus to highlight the miracle of his rising from the dead.

But those who have followed Jesus, putting their trust in him and his words, live out a range of emotions. Along with the shock and horror of reliving his gruesome death, they probably feel anger, disbelief and sadness. Who was this man, and why had they trusted him? What next?

On this day before the joy of the resurrection, take some time to place yourself imaginatively with the disciples (perhaps writing out the scene). Picture the setting—the sights and sounds. Discern what you are feeling as you move from one emotion to another. Ponder what sorts of conversations you have with your friends, and ask the Lord to speak any words he may have for you this day.

## Prayer

*Lord Jesus Christ, I can only imagine what the disciples felt the day after you died. Hope seemed to be extinguished along with your life. What had they trusted in? Why had they trusted in you? I too can feel this sense of disbelief when things don't turn out as I've hoped and prayed. I face disappointment, and often I blame you. When I don't understand, help me. Show me that you are the loving Lord who seeks to bless, even though I face trials and hardships while living in this fallen world. Turn my face to you, that I might know you and believe your goodness. On this day as we wait for the resurrection, give me the gift of empathy for those who face dire situations, that I might reach out in love.*

# Easter Day

# Forgiven and free

On the evening of that first day of the week, when the disciples were together, with the doors locked for fear of the Jewish leaders, Jesus came and stood among them and said, 'Peace be with you!' After he said this, he showed them his hands and side. The disciples were overjoyed when they saw the Lord.

Again Jesus said, 'Peace be with you! As the Father has sent me, I am sending you.' And with that he breathed on them and said, 'Receive the Holy Spirit. If you forgive anyone's sins, their sins are forgiven; if you do not forgive them, they are not forgiven.'…

Afterwards Jesus appeared again to his disciples, by the Sea of Galilee…

When they had finished eating, Jesus said to Simon Peter, 'Simon son of John, do you love me more than these?'

'Yes, Lord,' he said, 'you know that I love you.'

Jesus said, 'Feed my lambs.'

Again Jesus said, 'Simon son of John, do you love me?'

He answered, 'Yes, Lord, you know that I love you.'

Jesus said, 'Take care of my sheep.'

The third time he said to him, 'Simon son of John, do you love me?'

Peter was hurt because Jesus asked him the third time, 'Do you love me?' He said, 'Lord, you know all things; you know that I love you.'

Jesus said, 'Feed my sheep.'

JOHN 20:19–23; 21:1, 15–17

'Christ is risen! He is risen indeed! Alleluia!'

Joy comes in the morning, as we see in the resurrection accounts. The disciples reverberate with an amazed shock when they realise that Jesus lives, that he's been raised from the dead. They who had been huddling in a locked room, fearful of being persecuted by those in power, welcome his presence. When he breathes on them, filling them with the Holy Spirit, they receive peace, courage and strength. And note, when Jesus speaks his first words, some of them are on forgiveness: 'If you forgive anyone's sins, their sins are forgiven; if you do not forgive them, they are not forgiven' (John 20:23). The disciples are being prepared to spread the good news of salvation through the forgiveness of sins.

In the next chapter of John's Gospel, we see forgiveness in action as Jesus reinstates Peter. Three times had Peter denied him before the cock crowed, and now three times does Jesus ask if Peter loves him, telling him to feed Jesus' sheep. Peter no longer will be defined by his denials but as a forgiven person, free to minister in the name of his Lord. The church would not be the same without him: as we saw last week, he preached at Pentecost, urging those assembled to repent and receive the Holy Spirit; he exercised leadership, arranging for a disciple to replace Judas; he went on missionary journeys. As he lived out his call from God, he left behind the shame of his sinful actions. The Lord forgave him and restored him.

And that's the good news for us on this Resurrection Sunday. The Lord has been raised from the dead and he lives. Through his sacrificial death on the cross, he washes away our sins and wrongdoings when we repent. We no longer have to live out of our old self but can put on the clothes of the redeemed. We can wear our white robes with thankful hearts.

After the long season of Lent, we should celebrate the Easter season for more than just a day. If we celebrated for 40 days—up until the Ascension—our lives would be transformed. After all, celebration is one of the spiritual disciplines, even if many Christians overlook it, and what better to celebrate than the remission of our sins through our

Saviour's death and resurrection? By observing a celebratory season, we will be known for the joy that the Lord gives us, which keeps us buoyed in hope even during the difficult seasons.

Join me in some bubbly and a feast, including the best chocolate out there?[66]

'Christ is risen! He is risen indeed! Alleluia!'

## Prayer

*Loving Father, giving Son, comforting Spirit, thank you for journeying with us during Lent as we've explored the living cross and its gift of forgiveness and new life. Deepen in us our love for you and help us to live out of our new, redeemed selves. Thank you for the way you embody forgiveness and release of sins, so that we no longer have to be defined by them. May we continue to step forward in our callings, working for your glory in the ways you created us to do, which bring us joy and you pleasure. We're forgiven, Lord! Amen and alleluia.*

# Spiritual exercises and questions for individual reflection and group discussion

## Jesus' last week

As I mentioned on Palm Sunday, one way to approach Holy Week is to consider each day what Jesus experienced, being conscious throughout the day of the unfolding events. The following compilation is based on one found in the *NIV Application Commentary: Matthew*.[67]

### Saturday

- Evening celebration; Mary anoints Jesus (John 12:2–8)

### Sunday

- Entry into Jerusalem, with the crowds bearing palm branches (Matthew 21:1–11; Mark 11:1–10, John 12:12–18)
- Visit to the temple (Mark 11:11)
- Return to Bethany (Matthew 21:17; Mark 11:11)

### Monday

- Cursing the fig tree while going to Jerusalem (Matthew 21:18–22)
- Clearing the temple (Mark 11:15–17)
- Return to Bethany (Mark 11:19)

### Tuesday

- Reaction to the cursing of the fig tree while going back to Jerusalem (Mark 11:20–21)

- Debates with the religious leaders in Jerusalem and teaching in the temple (Matthew 21:23—23:39; Mark 11:27—12:44)
- Talk about future times on the Mount of Olives as they return to Bethany (Matthew 24:1—25:46; Mark 13:1–37)

## Wednesday

- Jesus and the disciples remain in Bethany
- Judas returns to Jerusalem to plan for his betrayal of Jesus (Matthew 26:14–16; Mark 14:10–11)

## Thursday

- Preparations for Passover (Matthew 26:17–19; Mark 14:12–16)
- Passover meal and Last Supper (Matthew 26:20–35; Mark 14:17–26)
- Farewell discourse with his disciples (John 13—17)
- Praying in the garden of Gethsemane (Matthew 26:36–46; Mark 14:32–42)

## Friday

- Perhaps in the very early hours, betrayal by Judas and arrest (Matthew 26:47–56; Mark 14:43–52)
- Jewish trial—three phases: appearing before Annas (John 18:13–24), before Caiaphas and part of the Sanhedrin (Matthew 26:57–75; Mark 14:53–65), and before the fully assembled Sanhedrin (Matthew 27:1–2; Mark 15:1)
- Roman trial—three phases: appearing before Pilate (Matthew 27:2–14; Mark 15:2–5), Herod Antipas (Luke 23:6–12) and Pilate again (Matthew 27:15–26; Mark 15:6–15)
- Crucifixion (Matthew 27:27–66; Mark 15:16–39)

## Sunday

- Witnesses to the resurrection (Matthew 28:1–8; Mark 16:1–8; Luke 24:1–12)

- Resurrection appearances (Matthew 28:9–20; Luke 24:13–52; John 20—21)

## Swords to the cross

You will need a palm cross.

On Palm Sunday, many churches give out palm crosses. These can be useful for thinking about the evil in the world and how God has overcome it through Jesus' death on the cross.

Hold your cross as if it were a sword, with the long end pointing outwards. As you do, pray for nations in the world which you know are suffering from war, bloodshed and oppression. Think of ways that you've held a sword out against others, perhaps through piercing words or a sulking stare.

As you move the cross back into its standing position, meditate on this verse and pray for forgiveness: 'For God was pleased to have all his fullness dwell in him, and through him to reconcile to himself all things, whether things on earth or things in heaven, by making peace through his blood, shed on the cross' (Colossians 1:19–20).[68]

## Writing in the sand

You will need a bowl or dish; sand.

Run your fingers through the sand, considering the grains and how many there are in just a small handful. Think about the promise God made to Abraham that he would be the father of many nations, as countless as the sand on the seashore. Then ponder the story about the woman accused of adultery and how Jesus wrote in the sand. What do you think he was writing?

Smooth out the sand and write with your finger (in shorthand, if necessary) a sin or sins you'd like to release to the Lord. It could be your own wrongdoing or the sins committed against a group of people by others. Ask the Lord to show you how to pray. When you have finished writing, picture the cross and how Jesus' sacrifice takes away our sin. Smooth out the sand, knowing that you are forgiven and free.

## The Last Supper

You will need a copy of a painting of the Last Supper. (Leonardo da Vinci's is the most famous, but others can be found online.)

If you have time, read the account of the last supper that Jesus ate with his friends, from John 13:1—14:7. Thinking prayerfully about Jesus' words to his friends, gaze at the painting. What stands out to you? What do you notice? Which point in the evening does the artist capture? Does your understanding of Jesus' final meal with his friends change as you ponder it?[69]

## Nail it

You will need a nail; a hammer; a cross made of two pieces of wood; paper and pen.

We return to the first exercise from Week 1, again bringing our wrongdoings to the living cross. Write on a piece of paper any fresh or lingering sins that you want to bring to Jesus for forgiveness. This time, nail the folded paper to the cross, knowing that Jesus' death brings you release. Receive God's love and forgiveness.

Alternatively, use a nail in your prayers, holding it (carefully) and considering how nails have been used—for building houses and for destroying our Saviour. How does God want to speak to you through this object?

# Questions for reflection and discussion

- Have you ever experienced a 'crowd mentality', when people's emotions change violently under the pressure of others? How much of this psychology do you think lies behind the crowd's change of attitude—from laying palms in adulation at the feet of Jesus to calling for his death?
- Which part of the parable of the lost son speaks most deeply to you? Why?
- What persecution of Christians do you see around the world today? Does the fact that Jesus warned his disciples not to be surprised by it make it easier to witness? Why or why not?
- What does Holy Communion mean to you? How would you like to enlarge that meaning?
- Peter was restored, forgiven for his betrayal. How do you think he felt? How do you feel when you're forgiven?
- What has struck you most deeply this Holy Week?
- How will you live differently following this extended journey into the theme of forgiveness? How has the cross come alive for you?

# Acknowledgements

I give thanks for:

The encouragement many years ago of Naomi Starkey, then commissioning editor for BRF, for me to write this book.

The gentle championing by Karen Laister, BRF wonder woman; the grace, forbearance and wisdom of my gentleman editor, Mike Parsons; and the many corrections Lisa Cherrett made in her copyedit.

My lovely cover designer, Vivian Hansen, who came up with just the right illustration and design.

My writing group, where I squeal with frustration and delight and where I receive profound encouragement and feedback.

My early readers, who provided valuable constructive criticism, saving me from misunderstandings and gaffes and spurring me along.

My prayer warriors, who support me and encourage me and drop me a line at just the right time.

The friends who provided a spacious bolt-hole in which to write uninterrupted.

My family who understand when I'm under deadline and who wait patiently for me to finish, always cheering me on with love.

# For further reading

## Christian explorations of forgiveness

R.T. Kendall, *Total Forgiveness* (Hodder, 2001).
R.T. Kendall, *Totally Forgiving Ourselves* (Hodder, 2007).
R.T. Kendall, *Totally Forgiving God* (Hodder, 2012).
    Modern classics on three vital aspects of forgiveness.

Russ Parker, *Forgiveness is Healing* (DLT, 1993).
    A guide to exploring the healing nature of forgiveness through
    the work of the Holy Spirit.

Miroslav Volf, *Free of Charge: Giving and forgiving in a culture stripped of grace* (Zondervan, 2005).
    An excellent look at giving and forgiving from a theologian who
    writes engagingly, including from his own life growing up in
    Croatia.

## For theological background

I love Bible commentaries, and my favourite series is one that
Zondervan was publishing when I worked there as an editor: 'The
NIV Application Commentaries'. Renowned Bible scholars do biblical
exegesis along with applying the biblical principles to our life today.
Some of the applications may feel a bit dated now, even just 15–20
years after publication, but I still highly recommend this series. The
other series I recommend is IVP's 'The Bible Speaks Today'.

Anthony Bash, *Just Forgiveness: Exploring the Bible, weighing the issues*
(SPCK, 2011).

Christof Gestrich, *The Return of Splendor in the World: The Christian
doctrine of sin and forgiveness* (Eerdmans, 1997). Translated by Daniel

W. Bloesch from *Die Wiederkehr des Glanzes in der Welt*, 1989 (J.C.B. Mohr [Paul Siebeck], 1989).

L. GregoryJones, *Embodying Forgiveness: A theological analysis* (Grand Rapids, MI: Eerdmans, 1995).

Lord Longford, *Forgiveness of Man by Man* (Buchebroc Press, 1989).

Fraser Watts and Liz Gulliford (eds), *Forgiveness in Context: Theology and psychology in creative dialogue* (T&T Clark, 2004).

## Stories of forgiveness

Ray Norman, *Dangerous Love: A true story of tragedy, faith, and forgiveness in the Muslim world* (Nelson, 2015).
The story of a father and daughter being shot at close range amid the sand dunes in Mauritania, and how he and his family forgive the perpetrator, even travelling to the prison to meet him.

Robin Oake, *Father, Forgive* (Authentic Media, 2008).
Not only the story of how Robin Oake forgave the one who killed his police-officer son, but a theological consideration of forgiveness.

Terri Roberts with Jeanette Windle, *Forgiven: The Amish school shooting, a mother's love, and a story of remarkable grace* (Bethany House, 2015).
Another side of a mass-murderer story—that of Terri Roberts, the mother of the one who committed the atrocity. Her son shot ten Amish girls, murdering five before he killed himself.

## Other views on forgiveness

Marina Cantacuzino, *The Forgiveness Project: Stories for a vengeful age* (Jessica Kingsley Publishers, 2015).
Stories from around the world detailing how people have forgiven.

Desmond Tutu and Mpho Tutu, *The Book of Forgiving* (Collins, 2014).
A psychological approach in a self-help manual on how and when to forgive.

Simon Wiesenthal, *The Sunflower: On the possibilities and limits of forgiveness* (Schocken, 1969, 1998).
An SS officer asks a Jewish prisoner to forgive him. The original story of the prisoner along with over 50 responses by theologians, activists, Holocaust survivors and others.

# Notes

1 Simon Wiesenthal, *The Sunflower: On the possibilities and limits of forgiveness* (Schocken, 1969, 1998), p. 27. The following quotations all come from this first chapter. To avoid an overabundance of notes, they are pages 30, 33, 42, 53, 54 and 54–55.

2 I've followed the order of the biblical books in moving from the Old Testament to the New.

3 I first came across an abbreviated version quoted in Timothy Radcliffe, *Seven Last Words* (Burns & Oates, 2004), p. 19; he attributes it to St John Chrysostom. I found the fuller quotation online, attributed to an unknown fifth-century writer: 'Cosmic Tree-Pseudo Chrysostom', *Crossroads Initiative*, 8 Feb 2016, www.crossroadsinitiative.com/media/articles/cosmic-tree-pseudo-chrysostom (accessed 3 August 2016).

4 Such as with ancient marriage contracts, as outlined in John H. Walton, *NIV Application Commentary: Genesis* (Zondervan, 2001), pp. 445–46. For a more in-depth look, see David Instone-Brewer, *Divorce and Remarriage in the Bible: The social and literary context* (Eerdmans, 2002).

5 See M. Stoll, *Birth in Babylonia and the Bible: Its Mediterranean setting* (Styx, 2000).

6 Anthony Bash makes this latter point in *Just Forgiveness: Exploring the Bible, weighing the issues* (SPCK, 2011), p. 19. See also Lord Longford's chapter 'The Jewish approach to forgiveness' in his *Forgiveness of Man by Man* (Buchebroc Press, 1989), pp. 15–20.

7 I'm indebted to Walton for this interpretation in *Genesis*, pp. 689–90.

8 Robin Oake, *Father, Forgive* (Authentic Media, 2008), p. 19.

9 I found the idea for this exercise at http://cup-a.blogspot.co.uk/2012/02/anticipating-easter-lent-and-sweet.html (accessed 3 August 2016).

10 This exercise is inspired by Wendy Rayner and Annie Slade, *Multi-Sensory Seasons* (SU, 2005), p. 16.

11 Bill T. Arnold, *NIV Application Commentary: 1 Samuel* (Zondervan, 2003), p. 131.

12 Arnold, *1 Samuel*, p. 132.

13 Arnold, *1 Samuel*, p. 132.

14  Many people find this story difficult, and understandably so. How could a good God order the destruction of these people? Do we see only a God of wrath in the Old Testament? For a look at the issues in more depth, see, for instance, John Allister, 'The Amalekite genocide' in *The Briefing*, 12 August 2013, http://matthiasmedia.com/briefing/2013/08/the-amalekite-genocide (accessed 3 August 2016).

15  As argued persuasively in Arnold, *1 Samuel*, pp. 536–37.

16  Of course I'm a participant in a foreign marriage! But now, with the Holy Spirit dwelling in God's people, we can marry outside our nationality while staying in the family of God and not being drawn to apostasy and syncretism, which is what the Lord was seeking to keep his people from.

17  Background information gleaned from Gerald H. Wilson, *NIV Application Commentary: Psalms Volume 1* (Zondervan, 2002), pp. 545–46.

18  Inspired by 'Scars' in Sue Wallace, *Multi-Sensory Worship* (SU, 2009), pp. 32–33.

19  I found the idea for the wipe-clean board in Claire Daniel, *80 Creative Prayer Ideas* (BRF, 2014), pp. 130–31.

20  Russ Taff sings the version running through my head on his album *Under Their Influence* (Mep/Royal Music, 1991).

21  I'm indebted to Charles L. Feinberg, *The Expositor's Bible Commentary: Jeremiah* (Zondervan, 1986), p. 498, for this understanding.

22  Michael Carl, 'Ugandan President repents of personal, national sins', *WND*, 24 November 2012, www.wnd.com/2012/11/ugandan-president-repents-of-personal-national-sins/#1S7v4BsvF5XRcy4f.99 (accessed 3 August 2016).

23  'The Program', *The Two Strike Hitter: Adultery, redemption and finding your way home*, http://twostrikehitter.weebly.com/blog/the-program (accessed 3 August 2016).

24  The first year was the hardest. I share some of the joys and the aches of finding myself on this side of the Atlantic in *Finding Myself in Britain: Our search for faith, home and true identity* (Authentic Media, 2015).

25  Many people struggle over whether this really happened, wondering if Jonah is a parable. James Bruckner, in his introduction to *NIV Application Commentary: Jonah* ( Zondervan, 2004), presents a strong case for us to suspend our disbelief.

26  Jonathan Langley, 'Can forgiveness be a tyranny? A conversation with Marina Cantacuzino', *Christian Today*, 19 September 2015, www.christiantoday.com/article/can.forgiveness.be.a.tyranny.a.discussion.with.marina.cantacuzino/64207.htm (accessed 3 August 2016).

27  Wilma Derksen in Marina Cantacuzino, *The Forgiveness Project: Stories for a vengeful age* (Jessica Kingsley, 2015), p. 116.

28  Cantacuzino, *Forgiveness Project*, pp. 116–17.

29  Full-orbed forgiveness, of course, includes our salvation through Jesus and his death on the cross. Common grace is no substitute for salvific grace.

30  Inspired by Daniel, 'God's love', in *80 Creative Prayer Ideas*, pp. 138–39.

31  Russ Parker says that the same Greek word is used for both freedom and release, and that it's one of the standard words for forgiveness in the New Testament. Thus we could argue that the Lord comes to 'proclaim forgiveness to the prisoners'. See Russ Parker, *Forgiveness is Healing* (DLT, 1993), pp. 7–8.

32  The title of the fine book by Russ Parker referenced above: *Forgiveness is Healing*.

33  See an interview with a Johns Hopkins psychiatrist, Karen Swartz: Lauren Sandler, 'The healing power of forgiveness', *Johns Hopkins Medicine*, 25 (summer 2014), www.hopkinsmedicine.org/news/publications/johns_hopkins_health/summer_2014/the_healing_power_of_forgiveness (accessed 3 August 2016).

34  For this historical background I'm indebted to Michael J. Wilkins, *The NIV Application Commentary: Matthew* (Zondervan, 2004), pp. 248–55.

35  We trust the Lord for wisdom, for of course it's not wise to seek reconciliation if the offending party has no desire or will to change.

36  We're 61 per cent the way through, actually. My husband and son will love this precision.

37  R.T. Kendall, *Total Forgiveness* (Hodder, 2001), p. 70. See also the other two excellent books in the trilogy: *Totally Forgiving Ourselves* (Hodder, 2007) and *Totally Forgiving God* (Hodder, 2012).

38  For instance, Wilkins, *Matthew*, p. 280.

39  See her book: Terri Roberts with Jeanette Windle, *Forgiven: The Amish school shooting, a mother's love, and a story of remarkable grace* (Bethany House, 2015).

40  Background information gleaned from Darrel L. Bock, *The NIV Application Commentary: Luke* (Zondervan, 1996), pp. 218–19.

41  Wilkins, *Matthew*, p. 636.

42  Wilkins, *Matthew*, p. 637.

43  Wilkins, *Matthew*, p. 637.

44  Part of this prayer is based on 1 Peter 3:15–16.

45    Rev Dr Anthony Harvey, sub-dean of Westminster, gave the address to the congregation. 'Martyrs of the modern era', *BBC News*, 9 July 1998, http://news.bbc.co.uk/1/hi/uk/129587.stm (accessed 3 August 2016).

46    Quoted in Karen Millington, *Is Forgiveness Always Possible?*, BBC Religion & Ethics, 20 December 2013, www.bbc.co.uk/religion/0/24986104 (accessed 3 August 2016).

47    James Bryan Smith, *Hidden in Christ: Living as God's beloved* (Hodder, 2014), p. 146.

48    Smith, *Hidden in Christ*, p. 146.

49    Smith, *Hidden in Christ*, p. 146.

50    Based on Colossians 3:1–14.

51    Ellen Crossman, *Mountain Rain: A personal story of total dependence on God* (Authentic Media/OMF, 1982), pp. 89, 91–92.

52    I'm conscious that I've mentioned unanswered prayer only briefly. It's a huge topic, and one that can be troubling. The best book on unanswered prayer I've read is Pete Greig, *God on Mute: Engaging the silence of unanswered prayer* (Kingsway, 2007).

53    Jerome, *On Galatians*, VI.10, quoted in David Jackman, *The Message of John's Letters* (IVP, 1988), p. 11.

54    William Batchelder Bradbury added to Anna Bartlett Warner's poem and added the musical arrangement in 1862.

55    See my *Finding Myself in Britain*, which looks at the UK in a through-the-year approach and has two chapters on Lent and Easter.

56    I'm indebted to Wilkins, *Matthew*, pp. 286–87 for the historical background.

57    Imaginative prayer was first most famously advocated by Ignatius of Loyola, who founded the Jesuits in the 16th century.

58    Victor Hugo, *Les Misérables*, trans. Lee Fahnestock and Norman MacAfee (Signet, 1987), p. 106, as quoted in Miroslav Volf, *Free of Charge: Giving and forgiving in a culture stripped of grace* (Zondervan, 2005), p. 204.

59    See, for example, Bruce Milne, *The Message of John* (IVP, 1993), p. 124.

60    Milne, *The Message of John*, p. 124.

61    Carol Kuruvilla, 'Why forgiveness is at the center of faith for this black pastor', *HuffPost Voices*, 26 October 2015, www.huffingtonpost.com/entry/forgiveness-faith-black-pastor_us_5626aa13e4b0bce34702c044 (accessed 3 August 2016).

62    Merrill C. Tenney, *The Expositor's Bible Commentary: John*, Vol. 9 (Zondervan, 1981), p. 157.

63  We can extend forgiveness while still seeing the perpetrators prosecuted and punished for their crimes. Forgiveness doesn't mean that we abandon seeking justice under the law. Yet forgiveness might also mean that we decide not to pursue a legal claim, letting go of, say, a minor civil offence as we acknowledge that God forgives us our sins.

64  Jennifer Rees Larcombe, *Journey into God's Heart: The true story of a life of faith* (Hodder, 2006), p. 269.

65  Rees Larcombe, *Journey into God's Heart*, p. 269.

66  Fairly traded, of course.

67  Wilkins, *Matthew*, pp. 709–10.

68  This exercise is inspired by Julia McGuinness, *Creative Praying in Groups* (SPCK, 2005), pp. 125–26.

69  Inspired by Wendy Rayner and Annie Slade, *Multi-Sensory Seasons* (SU, 2005), p. 23.

Amy Boucher Pye is an author and speaker who has written *Finding Myself in Britain: Our search for faith, home & true identity* (Authentic Media, 2015). She runs the *Woman Alive* book club and enjoys writing devotional thoughts for *New Daylight* and *Day by Day with God*, among others. She blogs regularly at amyboucherpye.com.